The Scrollsaw
Twenty Projects

To Jenny, my wife, for tolerating the trails of
sawdust around the house

The Scrollsaw

Twenty Projects

John Everett

Guild of Master Craftsman Publications Ltd

First published 1999 by
Guild of Master Craftsman Publications Ltd,
166 High Street, Lewes,
East Sussex, BN7 1XU

ISBN 1 86108 111 1

Cover photography by Anthony Bailey
Finished project photographs by Anthony Bailey
Step-by-step photographs by John Everett
Templates by John Everett
Scrollsaw diagram (page 3) by Simon Rodway

MEASUREMENTS
Although care has been taken to ensure that imperial measurements are true and
accurate, they are only conversions from metric. They have been rounded up and down to
the nearest reasonable fraction of an inch. Always check sizes before cutting

Designed by John Hawkins
Cover design by Wheelhouse Design
Typeface: Garamond
Colour origination by Viscan Graphics (Singapore)
Printed and bound by Kyodo Printing (Singapore) under
the supervision of MRM Graphics, Winslow, Buckinghamshire, UK

Contents

Introduction

Welcome to the scrollsaw project book that won't leave you wondering what to do next or how to do it. Whether you are a complete novice or an experienced scrollsaw enthusiast, you should feel confident tackling the designs in this collection. Each project is fully described with step-by-step pictures, text and drawings which follow through the construction of each piece.

The projects contained in this book have been carefully selected so that you can gain experience of different scrollsaw techniques as you work your way through it. Each project has been chosen so that only the very minimum amount of tools and equipment, other than the scrollsaw itself, are needed, bearing in mind that most of us don't have access to a large, expensively equipped workshop. The various items which will come in useful are outlined in the chapter on tools and equipment, together with a brief outline of some of the more useful types of scrollsaw blades.

Most of the pieces can be easily adapted to suit your own preferences in terms of size, and type of material used in their construction. You may well have a prized piece of timber you are waiting to use, or you may wish to make up a design to fit in a particular space in your home.

Whatever your own individual needs, you can adapt these designs to fit.

The step-by-step photographs for each project were taken during the actual construction, to show how pieces go together and in what order things should happen. The photographs were taken during the sawing, gluing and other activities which go to make up a completed project, so there is sawdust and waste material in some of the pictures. No attempt has been made to clean up. Tidying up was only done where it was important for clarity, to show what should be happening in the picture.

When you are ready to begin a project, read through the text and look at the pictures and drawings to familiarize yourself with what will be needed to complete each project. This will not only save you time later on, it will help you avoid making inconvenient errors. Once you are happy that you have an image of what you need to do in your mind, you should have no difficulty in successfully completing your chosen project.

Above all, scrollsawing should be a rewarding experience, and with a little patience and practice, getting used to how the scrollsaw works best, everyone can achieve worthwhile results with this versatile machine.

CHAPTER 1

Tools and equipment

Nowadays, the terms scrollsaw and fretsaw are applied without distinction to virtually any powered saw that takes thin blades. Strictly speaking there is a difference between the two types of machine, but with the advent of adapter kits, which allow the use of pin-end or plain-end blades in either type of saw, and incorporate a quick-change blade facility, more usually associated with the fretsaw, there seems little point in being pedantic. Both types of machine will carry out the same job – making intricate cuts in wood and other materials – so choosing a saw really depends on the more practical aspects of what the machine will be expected to accomplish for the user.

There are many different makes and type of saw available, so it is really a matter of selecting the machine which suits your requirements. The main advantage of scrollsaws and fretsaws is that they can make intricate cuts. Most, if not all, types of saw will manage this function well. However, the quality of engineering that has gone into each machine, and the facilities a particular make or model has to offer, differs from machine to machine, as does the price.

The following section offers a brief guide to the scrollsaw and what you should look for when buying one.

WHAT TO LOOK FOR

A few general pointers about what to look for when buying a new fretsaw or scrollsaw. Many saws are purchased by mail order, or with the buyer being handed a pre-packed carton in a DIY store, so it is difficult to know for sure whether or not you are buying the right machine for your purposes. If you are at the point of buying a saw for the first time, or are intending to replace an ageing saw, take the time to check the equipment reviews in woodworking magazines. Most magazines will provide back numbers if asked.

1 Look for a well-engineered machine with, preferably, no side play in the blade-carrying arms, both top and bottom.

2 Make sure the saw has a large enough throat capacity to cope with projects you envisage undertaking with the saw. The most generally available throat capacity is 406mm (16in). There is, of course, always the option of using a spiral blade for the occasional larger project, so do not feel you have to buy an industrial size machine just to gain extra throat capacity unless you will need it on a fairly regular basis.

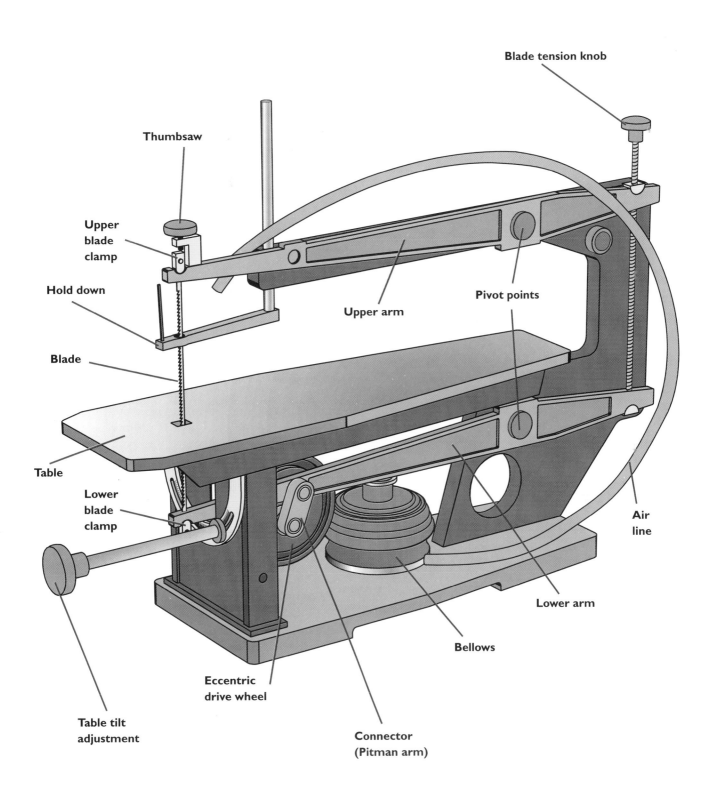

Blade tension knob

Thumbsaw

Upper blade clamp

Hold down

Blade

Table

Lower blade clamp

Table tilt adjustment

Eccentric drive wheel

Connector (Pitman arm)

Bellows

Lower arm

Air line

Pivot points

Upper arm

3 A variable cutting speed is a useful facility. The majority of saws have either one or two speeds, with a variable speed control as an optional extra. This feature is usually fitted at the factory and must be ordered with the saw. A simple alternative, which will be invaluable if you intend cutting thin sheet materials, such as Perspex, is to buy a drill speed controller and connect it between your saw and the power supply. This will give you a full range of speeds, from very slow to maximum, at a fraction of the cost of a factory supplied device. You can also use a speed controller on any other machine you own, within the limits of the controller itself, which means you can keep the speed controller if you decide to buy another saw.

4 If you do not already have a saw, and wish to use a full range of both pin-end and plain-end blades, check that the saw you want can either already accept both types of blade, or can be supplied with an adapter kit.

5 With many scrollsaw projects there will be a number of internal cutouts

to make, so a quick-change blade facility is essential. There is nothing worse than wrestling with a hex screw arrangement when you have to fit and remove a blade several times to make a number of internal cutouts. There are several independent companies now making quick-change blade adapter kits for most makes of saw. Their details can usually be found in the woodworking magazines.

6 Some types of saw, typically the more traditional scrollsaws, have blade holders which consist of a solid block of steel with a slot for the blade, clamped by a hex screw with a shaped underside to allow it to rock on a groove in the saw arm, and thus remain upright. They usually have a metal guard to prevent the blocks flying off in the event of a blade breakage. Unless you only intend using the saw very occasionally, avoid this design as it is thoroughly impractical for most modern scrollsaw work. By far the best types of blade holder pivot on a bearing of some sort, attached to the saw arms, and have a quick-change blade holding arrangement effected by a

▼ *Below* A typical scrollsaw

▶ *Below right* Fitting the blade on the Rexon scrollsaw using the T wrench provided with the machine.

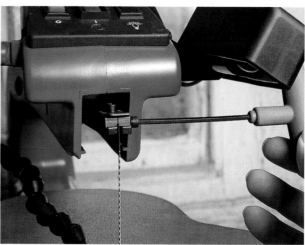

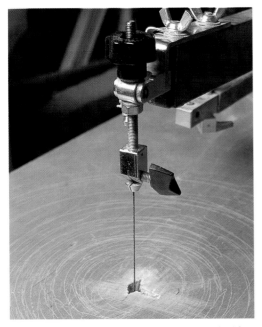

▲ The quick-change blade holders which make life easier when making internal cutouts.

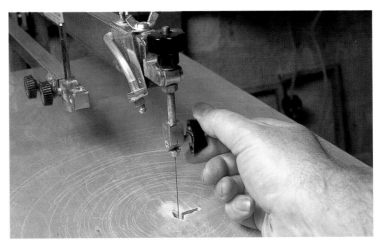

▲ Securing a blade on the Diamond machine with the quick-release key which is built into the blade holder.

thumbscrew. These blade holders are much quicker and easier to use and do not suffer from the problems of the older type of design. Even if you already possess a saw of the older type you can easily upgrade to a far more convenient arrangement using an adapter kit.

7 The scrollsaw should run at its fastest speed with a minimum of vibration. This may sound obvious, but a vibrating saw can blur the fine line of a cutting pattern and lead to cutting inaccuracies, as well as producing a poor quality of cut edge. Many saws will rely on being bolted down to a bench to achieve optimum stability when in use. This is fine as long as it doesn't mean that engineering quality of the saw has been compromised in order to keep the price down. The saw should not rely on efficient clamping to hide poor design and build.

BLADES

There are a huge variety of blade types available. They are, like most things, available in various qualities. It is always advisable to go for a good quality blade as it will not only last far longer than a cheap one, it will give a cleaner cut edge to the workpiece. The different types of blade available fall into several categories.

Certain kinds of scrollsaw take pin-end blades of a somewhat coarser nature than the fretsaw, which traditionally uses plain-end blades, and can accept blades of the finest grades made. Most scrollsaws now accept either type of blade. If you have a scrollsaw which will only accept pin-end blades, you might want to consider fitting one of the adapter kits which permit the use of either pin-end or plain-end blade.

Plain-ended blades are available in all sizes. Pin-ended blades are available in the medium to larger sizes only. There are a similar range of sizes in spiral, skip-tooth and reverse-tooth blades. Similarly numbered blades may vary quite a bit from manufacturer to manufacturer. They will all have the same number of teeth per centimetre, but the

Blade no.	Teeth per cm	Purpose
00	11.0	Finer sawing tasks such as veneers and thin plastic sheet
0	9.5	As above
1	9.0	As above
2	8.5	Tight turning cuts in hardwood up to 12mm (½in) thick and softwood up to 20mm (¾in)
3	7.0	As above
4	6.25	As above
5	5.5	Tight turning cuts in hardwood up to 20mm (¾in) in thickness and softwood up to 25mm (1in)
6	5.0	As above
7	4.75	General cutting hardwood up to 25mm (1in) in thickness and softwood to 35mm (1⅜in)
8	4.5	As above
9	4.25	As above
10	4.0	General cutting in hardwood up to 35mm (1⅜in) in thickness and softwood up to 50mm (2in)

A selection of blades that can be fitted to a scrollsaw. From the top they are:

▶ Tungsten carbide tile cutting blade. An extraordinary accuracy and speed of cutting can be obtained using this blade, which can be of particular benefit to the DIY tiler.

▶ No. 12 scrollsaw blade, suitable for fast cutting of pine and other softwoods.

▶ No. 7 skip-tooth blade, which is used mainly to cut man-made sheet material such as MDF and plywood.

▶ No. 7 spiral blade. This blade has teeth all the way round and can be used to cut in any direction.

▶ No. 3 skip-tooth blade. This is a much finer blade for cutting very thin material accurately.

▶ No. 3 fret blade. A very fine-toothed blade for sawing veneers.

performance will vary considerably. Try several makes and settle on one which suits your own way of working the best.

General purpose

General purpose blades are available in a range of sizes with either pin-ends or plain-ends. These blades are intended for cutting most thicknesses of wood. The size of blade you use will depend on the thickness of wood and the tightness of curve to be cut. Blades are numbered according to the coarseness of pitch of the cutting teeth, i.e. a No. 12 blade will be pretty coarse, while a No. 4 blade will be fine, with more teeth per centimetre.

Skip-tooth blades

These have, as the name implies, a gap between the teeth where, in effect, a tooth is missing. Skip-tooth blades are intended for use with man-made boards and sheet material, such as plywood and MDF. They cut this material more efficiently than a normal blade because their cutting action causes less friction and therefore less heating of the workpiece. This is essential when cutting man-made materials which use glue in their manufacture. The lower friction of a skip-tooth blade means that the blade does not clog with glue, as it would with a normal blade. These blades are available in a range of sizes just like general purpose blades.

Spiral blades

This is another very useful blade which permits cutting in any direction, without having to rotate the workpiece. This means that very large pieces can be

worked on with a small capacity scrollsaw because there is no need to turn the workpiece in the usual way to follow the cutting line on the pattern. Again, these blades are available in a variety of sizes.

There are many other blade types available, including some special purpose blades for cutting almost anything you can think of – from glass to house bricks! It is well worth playing around with a few of the more common blade types to get a feel for what they can achieve, in terms of suitable cutting speed, coping with tight bends and producing good clean cuts in a variety of materials. This way you can gain practical experience of your equipment, which is worth more than all the theories put together.

DRILL AND DRILL BITS

A drill and a selection of bits is essential. Whether the drill is electric or hand operated does not matter much as long as you can drill starter holes, for threading scrollsaw blades, as well as pilot and clearance holes for fixing screws and panel pins.

A small set of metric drill bits up to about 5mm in diameter, or imperial measurements of up to about ¼in, will be useful. A couple of the finer sizes for making nail pilot holes are handy, and will usually be included in most sets, particularly those sets of bits intended for mini-drills. A countersink bit is also essential, again many drill sets will have one of these included.

A couple of the smaller sizes of flat wood bits are useful, particularly for projects such as the wind vane which requires a clearance hole for a 12mm (½in) dowel.

DRILL SIZE TABLE

Screw gauge	Clearance holes		Pilot holes	
0	¹⁄₁₆in	1.5mm	¹⁄₃₂in	1.0mm
1	⁵⁄₆₄in	2.0mm	¹⁄₃₂in	1.0mm
2	⁵⁄₆₄in	2.0mm	³⁄₆₄in	1.0mm
3	³⁄₃₂in	2.5mm	¹⁄₁₆in	1.5mm
4	⁷⁄₆₄in	3.0mm	¹⁄₁₆in	2.0mm
5	⅛in	3.2mm	³⁄₃₂in	2.0mm
6	⁹⁄₆₄in	3.5mm	³⁄₃₂in	2.0mm
7	⁵⁄₃₂in	4.0mm	⁷⁄₆₄in	2.5mm
8	¹¹⁄₆₄in	4.5mm	⅛in	3.0mm
9	³⁄₁₆in	5.0mm	⅛in	3.5mm
10	¹³⁄₆₄in	5.0mm	⁹⁄₆₄in	3.5mm
12	⁷⁄₃₂in	5.5mm	⁹⁄₆₄in	4.0mm

All sizes are approximate and are satisfactory for most applications. Drill bit sizes are given as the closest commonly available sizes, as most of these drill bit sizes will be found in sets. Relatively obscure and difficult to find drill bit sizes have been omitted as that degree of precision is of no real benefit for woodworking in general.

JIGSAWS AND HANDSAWS

A further useful item is a power jigsaw for cutting out blanks. This is by no means essential as the more traditional handsaws are perfectly adequate for this type of task. If you have a power jigsaw, a blade suitable for cutting man-made sheet materials such as plywood and MDF, will be the most useful type to have installed.

MINIATURE FILES

A set of miniature files, such as those sold for modelmaking, will come in handy for cleaning up very tight areas, such as in intricate pattern parts, where it is difficult to get with a length of sandpaper.

BRUSH

It is a good idea to use a fairly stiff brush to remove the sawdust from around the cut edges of the workpiece. The sawdust tends to cling to the tight curves and can be a considerable nuisance when it comes to painting the piece. The sort of brush that is sold by stationers for cleaning typewriters, shaped like a pencil with a brush at one end and an eraser at the other, is ideal for this purpose and is inexpensive.

BENCH VICE

A bench vice of some sort can be useful for holding pieces, leaving both hands free to carry out any cleaning up or other operations that may be needed.

BLADE CONTAINER

There are some items which you can easily make for yourself, such as a quick-view blade container (see below). This can be made from scrap materials. A blade container will prove useful for holding your scrollsaw blades, allowing you to select the one you need quickly and easily. The one shown was made from an offcut of twin-wall acrylic sheet, the sort used for glazing greenhouses. This was mounted onto a scrap of wood and held in place with a couple of bracing strips. It could also be made from the plastic cores of fax paper rolls, with the appropriate size holes drilled into a base of scrap wood, or in any number of other ways. Use what you can find.

▲ A simple blade container allows quick and easy access to your stock of different scrollsaw blades.

PAINTING FRAME

A painting frame is useful when decorating some of the projects. Again, simplicity is the key. All that is required is a framework of battens pinned onto an old piece of hardboard or plywood, made water and paint proof with a layer of polythene, such as the side of a rubbish sack or a plastic carrier bag. Make the frame large enough to accommodate the biggest panel you intend to paint, although the construction of the frame is cheap enough to allow you to make a couple of different sizes if you wish.

DRYING RACK

Another handy item if you have space for it, is a drying rack. This again is just a wooden frame mounted horizontally on a base of some sort, so that short pieces of wire, cut from a wire coat hanger, can be used to support painted items while they dry. A little ingenuity can provide custom-made frames for almost any similar purpose.

ADDITIONAL TOOLS

Additional items you will find useful when tackling the projects in this book consist mostly of the commonly owned hand tools, such as a light hammer, screwdriver, files, which most people will already have in their toolbox.

CHAPTER 2

Materials

With an appropriate type of blade fitted, the scrollsaw can work its magic on most materials including paper and ceramic tiles. However, for the purposes of this book materials can be broadly divided into two main groups:

- natural timber, in all its varieties;
- man-made sheet material, such as plywood and MDF.

NATURAL TIMBER

Natural wood, that is sawn straight from a tree trunk, can be further sub-divided into softwood and hardwood. The scrollsaw will cope with all types of wood, but there are a few points worth remembering about the various kinds of wood normally available from suppliers.

Hardwood

Some hardwoods, such as oak, may have been fully cured some years prior to being used, so will have become extremely hard indeed. In this case, it would be better to use a metal-cutting blade rather than a standard variety.

Softwoods

Some pines and hemlocks are so soft that they leave a fibrous finish once sawn. With these types of timber, careful

► A selection of natural and man-made woods. From the bottom up: oak, mahogany, pine board, MDF and plywood.

sanding, particularly on the cut edges, may be required to get a smooth finish.

There are, of course, many different types of wood available and it is worth discussing your requirements with your supplier before deciding on which type of wood to use for any particular project.

MAN-MADE MATERIALS

One of the main groups of materials used extensively within the wood trade, and for many of the projects in this book, are the various types of plywood and MDF.

MDF (medium density fibreboard)

MDF is a mixture of wood fibres and glue rolled into sheets of varying thicknesses. The resulting 'wood' sheet is a versatile product, and can be used extensively for scrollsawing. As with chipboard, and other particle boards, fixing screws can be a problem, but this can often be overcome by using two different fixing methods, e.g. glue and screws, or glue and pins, or, indeed, by arranging things so that the fixings pass through the MDF and are secured into parts made from regular timber.

One of the convenient features of MDF, particularly for scrollsaw users, is the clean edge left on the material after cutting. Generally, MDF does not require any sanding, other than cleaning off saw tearout. This is a tremendous advantage when intricate and detailed work, which would be next to impossible to sand, is being cut. The face sides of MDF boards provide an adequate surface which does not need sanding. If any

mechanical damage has occurred, the board is usually inexpensive enough to just cut out any damaged section.

Another feature of sheet material, like MDF, is that it has no grain so that it cuts easily and at the same speed in any direction. Many woods, softwoods in particular, will cut much faster across the grain than along the grain. In conventional woodworking different saw blades are used for cutting across and with the grain of the wood, but this would be completely impractical for scrollsaw work which frequently uses intricate patterns, involving almost continuous switching from cutting across the grain to along the grain.

Plywood

Plywood is the other main sheet material used with the scrollsaw. This material is normally available in many different types and grades. Marine plywood, which is suitable for outside use, tends to be among the most expensive to buy, as is furniture grade birch plywood. Other types can be considerably cheaper, but, of course, they are not of such good quality, although this may not matter for many applications, such as the Hanging Basket Bracket (see page 74), where the item is going to be painted, so any imperfections, such as missing bits of wood, can easily be filled in before decorating.

The remaining characteristic of manmade sheet materials is the fact that they usually incorporate large quantities of glue in their manufacture. The glue can affect the more common types of saw blade, quickly clogging fine teeth and rendering them virtually useless. To counter this problem, a skip-tooth blade is normally used (see page 7).

OTHER MATERIALS

Ceramic tiles

There are many other materials which can be successfully cut on the scrollsaw by simply fitting the appropriate specialist blade. For instance, most scrollsaws, as well as many types of fretsaw, will accept pin-end blades. It is a simple matter to fit one of the tungsten carbide blades sold for cutting ceramic tiles, normally used in a small handsaw frame. With one of these in your scrollsaw, you can cut decorative shapes in ceramic tiles with both hands free to guide the tile quickly and easily. This makes cutting bits of broken tile for mosaics quick and easy. You can also use the same set-up for cutting old roofing slates down to $\frac{1}{12}$ scale for use on dolls' houses.

Perspex

Perspex (transparent acrylic sheet) can also be cut on the scrollsaw. This material usually comes with a protective anti-scratch sheet in place on both surfaces. Leave this in position until after you have completed your cutting to prevent the surface from being ruined with melted blobs of acrylic. You can also apply adhesive tape along your cutting line to prevent the same problem. Always cut Perspex at a slow speed to minimize melting.

Thick materials

Extra thick sections of wood and other materials can be cut up to the maximum capacity of your saw, as recommended by the maker. Remember that a thin blade with tiny teeth will take much longer to cut thicker material, so don't be in too much of a hurry. Never force the material into the blade, as this will distort the blade, preventing you from making a straight cut.

► Using oak of around 70mm (2¾in) in thickness to make some very substantial brackets. This thickness may well be a little beyond the capacity of most scrollsaws which usually have a 50mm (2in) maximum working thickness of material, but well illustrates the point that the scrollsaw can handle more than just thin sheets of material.

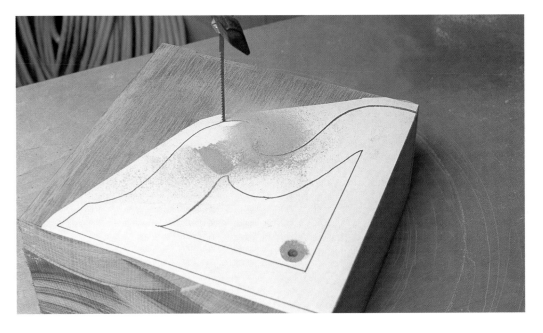

CHAPTER 3

Scrollsaw basics

MAKING A CUTTING PATTERN

A cutting pattern is simply a line drawing of the shape you intend to cut out, traced or copied to the size you need.

You may need to scale templates up or down. You can either do this on a photocopier, or you can scale up the template using a grid. You will find that some of the templates in this book, particularly decorative pieces, are arranged on a grid with the scale used marked at the bottom of the page. If the grid pattern is based on, say, a one centimetre grid, to create a 200% enlargement (double the original size), you would need to copy the template shape on a two centimetre grid.

- Number the rows of the grids on both the original and the copy, you will find it easier to find your place quickly.
- Put a dot at each point where the cutting line crosses from one square to another. All you then have to do is join the dots, ensuring any curves follow the lines of the original.
- You can sketch in the design first with a light pencil, as has been done in the example, before you commit yourself to an ink line, to get the drawing exactly right.

▲ Scaling up a template to make a cutting pattern.

Take your time making a satisfactory cutting pattern as the quality of the finished item will depend on the accuracy of this template. It is worth remembering the old woodworkers' saying 'measure twice and cut once'.

ATTACHING A CUTTING PATTERN

Attach the cutting pattern using an adhesive, such as spray mount, or other low-tack adhesive, which will allow the remains of the cutting pattern to be easily removed from the blank once cutting has been completed.

Try not to use too much adhesive when sticking the pattern to the blank or

▲ Attaching a cutting pattern to a blank using spray mount.

▼ *Below* Cutting out a marked-up blank with a jigsaw.

▶ *Below right* Sanding the saw tearout off a blank.

removing the pattern will prove messy. Once you get the hang of using spray mount, it is fairly easy to apply just the right amount of glue so you don't leave a sticky residue when the pattern is finally removed. Too little adhesive and the pattern won't stick properly, and will tend to ride up at the edges when you cut around it, making it difficult to follow the lines properly.

MAKING A BLANK

A blank is a plainly cut piece of wood or other material. It is usually cut a little larger than the size of the cutting pattern, so that there is some spare material which can be gripped to control the direction of the cut. If you wish to make rough blanks, make sure that you buy more material than indicated by the dimensions in the equipment and materials list in the project. That way you'll have plenty of additional material over and above the pattern size.

To make a blank, select the material you intend to use and place the cutting pattern on it in such a way as not to waste too much material.

- Draw around the outside of the cutting pattern – not too closely – marking out an area which is a little larger than the cutting pattern.
- Cut the blank free from its sheet with a saw. A jigsaw is useful if you have one, but any other suitable saw will do just as well.
- Sand off the edges of the material so that there is no saw tearout. Saw tearout is just the splinters which become raised as the saw cuts through the wood.

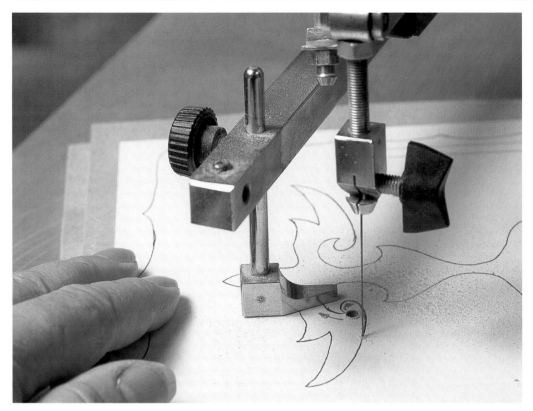

◄ Cutting under way with the hold down device correctly adjusted to prevent the workpiece 'chattering' when sharp turns are made.

SETTING UP THE SCROLLSAW

Before you start, make sure your scrollsaw is set up properly. Make sure it is bolted down to a firm bench. Check that the cables and plug are not damaged in any way, such as nicks in the insulation.

Some scrollsaws have an optional stand. This is a useful facility as it avoids having your workbench space taken up with tools and equipment. Some stands also have a built-in swivel chair for the operator. Whatever arrangement you end up with, make sure you are comfortable and relaxed.

The hold down device helps to keep the workpiece flat on the table, preventing 'chattering' when you turn corners with the saw. Make sure you set

the hold down device correctly before starting to saw.

The tension of the blade must be adjusted before you begin sawing. If the blade is too tight, there is a risk of breakage, too loose and the sawing line could become inaccurate. See the manufacturer's manual for details of how to adjust the tension on your saw.

BASIC CUTTING

Cutting with the scrollsaw is simple. You'll find that you improve with practice. Keep your eye on the point where the saw blade meets the cutting line and just follow the line. After a while you will be able to cut perfect straight lines and gentle curves, as well as the tight turns which the scrollsaw is so capable of.

▲ *Above* Using double-sided adhesive tape to attach two blanks together.

▶ *Above right* The cutting pattern attached to the top blank, ready for stack sawing.

STACK SAWING

Two or more identical pieces are achieved by a process known as stack sawing. Two or more blanks are simply fixed together, usually with double-sided adhesive tape, and sawn around at the same time. This makes the job much faster to complete, and ensures that all the pieces are identical.

- Just cut out the required number of blanks, and stick them together with little pieces of double-sided adhesive tape on the waste side of the cutting line.
- Attach the cutting pattern to the top blank.

- Cut around the cutting pattern. You may find that the blade cuts slightly slower because of the thickness of the material. Try not to force the material into the blade.

INTERNAL CUTOUTS

An internal cutout is a part of a pattern which needs to be cut away, but does not meet any of the edges, often forming part of the ornamentation of the piece.

To make an internal cutout you will need to drill a hole for the saw blade to pass through. If small, delicate cutouts are required, then you will need to use a drill bit not much larger than the width of your blade. If the cutout is not delicate, use a larger drill bit, to make threading the saw blades easier. Put a scrap of wood behind the hole position when you drill so you leave a clean edge at the back of the hole. This is particularly important if you are using plywood, as the splintering that can occur could spoil the final piece.

Try to drill the starter holes near a sharp point or angle on the design. This will make it easier to ensure that the beginning and end of the cut meet up

▼ The starter holes made at a point in the design where it will allow the cut to meet up easily.

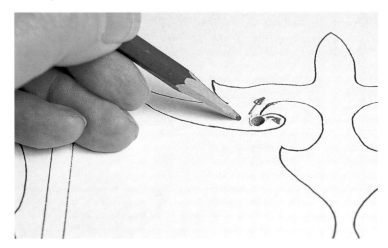

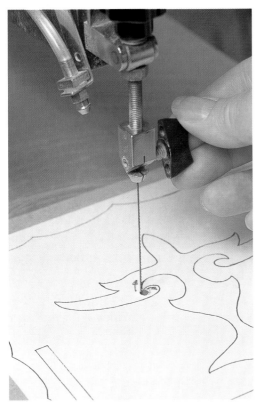

▲ Threading the blade through the starter hole and securing the blade in the top blade holder.

USING THE TILT TABLE

A tilting table facility on the scrollsaw allows you to cut at an angle. The bevel cut on the picture frame was made this way.

If your scrollsaw is not equipped with a worktable that can be set at different angles to allow bevel cutting, you can make a simple jig which can be clamped on top of the existing worktable to do the same job. You may find, depending on the design of your saw, that the maximum angle which can be obtained this way is limited by the position of the various components of your saw, typically the design and position of the top arm of the saw. You will, however, be able to cut bevels, even if you have to make do with an angle of less than 45 degrees.

▼ A Rexon saw showing the table tilting mechanism which has click stops at the most commonly used angles of tilt in addition to a scale.

easily. If you were to begin your cutting line along a straight or gently curving section of the pattern, the start and finish of the cut might not meet exactly, making intricate filing or sanding necessary to make the cutting line meet precisely.

Secure the blade in the saw's bottom blade holder first. Thread the blade through your starter hole and secure the blade in the top blade holder and tension it properly. Check the manufacturer's handbook for the particular tensioning arrangement for your saw.

It is usually better to complete the internal cutouts first. This will ensure that there is enough waste material to grip when guiding the blank along the cutting line.

MAKING A BEVEL CUTTING JIG

1 Cut a square of MDF or plywood, about 6mm (¼in) in thickness, to cover the width of your existing saw table. If your table is, for example, 300mm (11¾in) across, then you will need to cut a square with sides 300mm (11¾in) long.

2 Lay the square of material on your table and raise one side up, making a note where the highest point will be. This will probably be at an elevation of around 30 degrees. Check the angle with a protractor. Make sure the jig will not foul the top blade holder by making sure

the top blade holder is in its lowest working position, i.e. at the bottom of its travel. Make a note of the maximum angle you are going to be able to cut, remove the sheet from the table and mark the centre of the sheet.

3 Drill a hole, about 10mm (⅜in) in diameter, for the blade to pass through. A larger hole is needed because the blade will be cutting at an angle and so will need much more clearance than when cutting straight up and down.

4 Measure two pieces of MDF or plywood for the side panels of the jig. These can be of a thicker material

▼ Cross section of saw table with the bevel cutting jig in place.

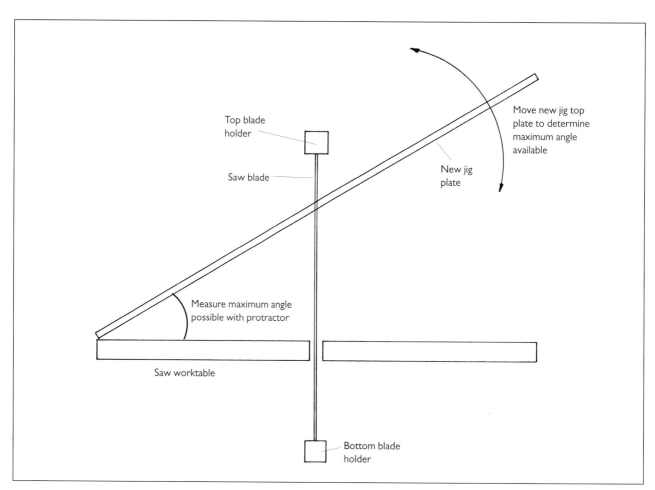

Top blade holder

Saw blade

Move new jig top plate to determine maximum angle available

New jig plate

Measure maximum angle possible with protractor

Saw worktable

Bottom blade holder

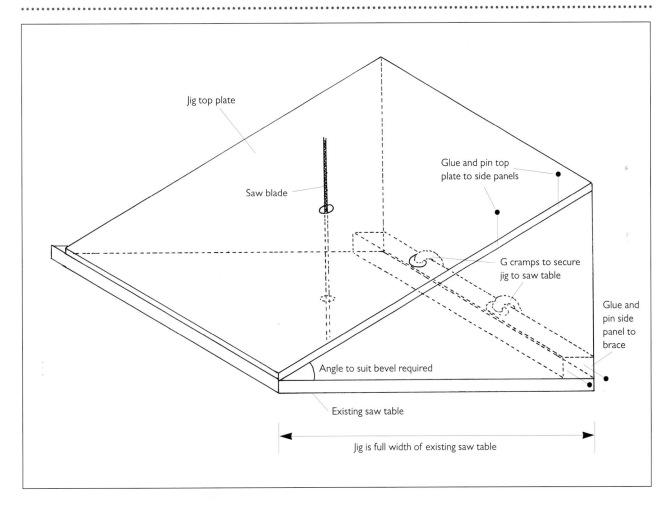

Jig top plate

Saw blade

Glue and pin top plate to side panels

G cramps to secure jig to saw table

Glue and pin side panel to brace

Angle to suit bevel required

Existing saw table

Jig is full width of existing saw table

▲ Completed jig with construction notes

than the top panel, because the thickness of the top sheet limits the maximum angle. The two side panels will need to be the width of your saw table, and cut according to the angle to be bevelled (limited by the maximum angle you can manage on your saw).

5 Secure the two side panels to the front and back edges of the top sheet. Glue and pin these, making sure they are perfectly upright, and leave the glue to harden thoroughly. When that is done, cut a brace from a piece of timber of around 50mm x 25mm (2in x 1in), to fit between the side panels of the jig at the base, where it will contact your existing saw table. Glue and pin this securely in place and allow the glue to set properly.

The bevel cutting jig should be clamped to your existing saw table with a couple of small G cramps. You use the top sheet of the jig as if it were your original saw table. You can make more than one of these jigs for different angles up to the maximum angle for your saw.

CHAPTER 4

Safety

It is easy to avoid safety problems with a little common sense.

WATCH YOUR HANDS

Always remember that, although the blades used in the scrollsaw or fretsaw are thin with tiny teeth, they are capable of cutting through thick, hard materials. This is a pretty good indication that, small though they may be, they are also perfectly capable of cutting through a finger or thumb. It is essential to keep an eye on where your fingers are in relation to the saw blade which you are cutting. This may seem obvious, but it is a point you should keep in mind while cutting out items on your saw.

▼ A typical dust mask – ideal for use when sawing MDF and other types of sheet material and wood which produces ultra-fine sawdust.

BLADE BREAKAGE

The majority of scrollsaw accidents occur when a blade breaks. The operator has usually been applying too much pressure to the workpiece to make it cut faster. Blades for the scrollsaw are not expensive, so if you find you need pressure to make the blade cut through your workpiece, change it. A replacement blade is considerably cheaper than a week or two off work with a damaged finger.

DUST MASKS

The tiny teeth of the scrollsaw produce such fine sawdust that it can remain suspended in the air for quite some time. This can be a considerable problem if not dealt with adequately and sensibly. Some materials, including a few hardwoods, produce dust which can have a toxic effect. Some man-made sheet materials, such as MDF, can also produce a similar reaction. This is a particular problem for those who suffer from asthma and other respiratory tract problems.

Many scrollsaws have a dust extraction facility underneath the saw table which is helpful, but, unfortunately not the complete answer to the problem. Even if you have a dust extractor on your machine, there will always be a fair

20

amount of dust produced above the saw table, which is why most saws also have an air blower to keep the line on your cutting pattern free of sawdust. When the blower is in operation, all the time you are sawing, the ultra-fine dust is blown into the air around you. This problem can be easily overcome by using a dust mask. It may seem obvious, but many scrollsaw users tend to try a dust mask and then discard it as uncomfortable or inconvenient. Spend a little time in finding a dust mask that is comfortable to wear. There are many different types and makes of dust mask readily available in most DIY stores and garages. Prevention is, after all, much better than cure.

Always clean up as much dust as possible when you have finished cutting with your scrollsaw. A build up of fine dust can clog the working parts of your scrollsaw. The application of good house-keeping will prevent such problems from occurring too often.

◄ Remember to switch off the saw before withdrawing from a cut.

CHAPTER 5

Finishing

There are as many possible wood finishes as there are types of wood. Some finishes require specialist skills and knowledge, such as french polishing. The more commonly available finishes, together with a few of the new craft products, are easy and safe to use, providing attractive finishes for all the projects in this collection. The finishes used in this book can be divided into three categories:

- Paint finishes and enamels.
- Decorative finishes. These cover a wide variety of effects ranging from marbling to crackle finishes. I used special effects for the mirror frame, collector's cabinet and the picture frames. These finishes work especially well on MDF.
- Wood stain and varnishes. These can be used to add colour, or to protect an item intended for outdoor use.

▼ A range of enamel paints

PAINT FINISHES

Whatever type of paint you are using, most woods, natural or artificial, will require some form of undercoat in order to get the best finish. There are exceptions to this of course, for instance if you want a distressed finish using emulsion paint. In general, however, the use of a good primer is not only an advantage, but in the case of some artificial materials such as MDF, virtually essential to obtain even paint coverage. A white primer not only seals the wood prior to painting so that the wood does not absorb too much paint, it also provides a degree of light reflection through the top coat of paint, giving the colour coat a brighter appearance.

Another advantage of using primer, particularly with soft woods and MDF, is that it renders immobile, and therefore removable with sandpaper, those annoying little bits that need to be sanded off but cannot be removed by sandpaper while the wood is bare.

Always allow the primer to dry thoroughly before attempting any further work on the piece. Acrylic primer usually only takes an hour to dry. Once fully dry, use fine sandpaper to get the surface smooth, ready for the top coat of paint.

If you plan to use enamel paints, such as Humbrol, for the colour coat make sure you use an acrylic primer, rather than an oil-based alternative. The oil-based version of the primer can react with the drying agents in the enamel paint, lengthening the drying time from a couple of hours to several days or more.

DECORATIVE FINISHES

Some decorative paint effect kits can be difficult to find locally, even if you have a craft shop nearby. There is a wide range of decorative effects available in a variety of makes. I used the beginner's kit, the smallest size supplied, which contains enough fluid to cover more than one decent-sized project.

The effects I used were designed to be applied with a sponge brush. However, in the absence of a local stockist of sponge brushes, and as they are comparatively expensive, a workable alternative is to buy an ordinary synthetic sponge and cut it to whatever size you want – you can have around twenty sponge brush equivalents for the price of just one sponge brush. You will need to use disposable rubber gloves, to prevent covering your hands with paint.

The kits I used were easy to use and fun to work with. The effects are totally realistic providing you follow the maker's instructions and are well worth trying even if only to see for yourself what they can do.

WOOD STAINS AND VARNISHES

Wood stains and varnishes can be applied to all natural woods by following the manufacturer's instructions.

MDF needs a special mention as it acts like a sponge, soaking up most solutions; wood stains and varnishes are no exception. If you want to stain MDF, the best approach is to apply the stain and let it dry completely. If you want to increase the depth of colour, apply a further coat and then let this dry. Once you are satisfied with the colour, apply the varnish as a separate coat on top. The heraldic shield house number project, cut from 6mm (¼in) MDF required four separate coats and a full two weeks to dry.

SAFETY NOTE

If the project you are making is to be used by children, make sure that the finish you apply is one of the non-toxic varieties. This information will always be carried on the container.

▼ A crackle paint effect kit.

THE PROJECTS

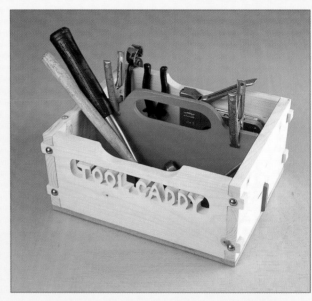

Mirror overlay

The mirror overlay design has butterflies in one pair of opposing corners, and oak leaves in the other corners. These are joined together with a fairly random design of tree branches, which makes the design simple to elongate or shorten to accommodate whatever size mirror you prefer. It is even possible to bend the design elements to frame an oval mirror.

If you are using a mirror size other than the 255mm x 200mm (10in x 8in) size used for the example, the whole design including the retaining frame and cover will need to be altered to suit your own mirror. This should not cause a problem, but do ensure the mirror retaining frame fits within the borders of the overlay, as shown on the template (see page 31).

EQUIPMENT AND MATERIALS

- Mirror, 255mm x 200mm (10in x 8in)
- 6mm (¼in) MDF sheet, size 280mm x 360mm (11in x 14⅛in), for the overlay
- 3mm (⅛in) MDF or plywood sheet, two pieces approximately 270mm x 220mm (10⅝in x 8¹¹⁄₁₆ in), for the retaining frame and securing panel
- 8 woodscrews, No. 2 10mm (⅜in), to fix the securing panel

- Drill bits, to drill pilot and clearance holes for woodscrews, see chart on page 8
- 2 screw eyes
- Suitable length of picture wire
- Wood glue
- Paints, varnish or stain of your choice. I used an antiquing kit to give an 'old' appearance.
- Spray mount or alternative, e.g. Cow gum
- Dust mask

1 Decide what size mirror you wish to use. Once you have chosen a mirror size, you can make up a cutting pattern based on the templates. To make a cutting pattern, draw the retaining frame to fit your own mirror. Scale the template of the overlay up or down, so that you have sufficient overlap of the design on the inside as well as the outside of the retaining frame. See page 13 for more details about scaling patterns.

The inside of the overlay also serves to prevent the mirror falling out, so you will need an adequate overlap over the edge of the mirror. Try to keep the retaining frame well within the dimensions of the overlay, so that it remains hidden from view once completed.

2 If you need to cut out a blank from a larger sheet of MDF, mark round your cutting pattern with a pencil and cut it to size. Use a jigsaw, or whatever you have available, to cut off the blank and sand off any saw tearout from the cut edges, to avoid snagging or binding once you transfer the blank to your scrollsaw.

3 Stick the cutting pattern in place on the MDF blank using spray mount.

4 The internal cutout should be made first to avoid putting undue strain on the MDF material, which can become brittle once it has been cut to relatively thin dimensions. Mark and drill a starter hole as shown. Thread your blade

through and secure it to your saw. Set the hold down device, if your saw has one, to prevent any 'chatter' as you turn corners during the cut. Put on your dust mask – essential when cutting MDF – and make the internal cut, following the lines of your cutting pattern carefully.

Once you have completed this cut, unfasten the blade from your saw and remove the workpiece from the table. Refit the blade to the saw ready for the external cut. The internal cut will create a good size piece of MDF material which can be retained for use on another project.

5 Make the external cut. Once completed, clear any remaining dust from the workpiece before removing the remains of your cutting pattern. You will notice that fine sawdust is produced, which is why a dust mask must be used. Remove the cutting pattern and sand off

▲ The scrollsaw blade threaded through the starter hole and the hold down positioned for the internal cutout.

► Gently sanding off the saw tearout from the back of the overlay sheet.

▼ The cutting pattern positioned ready for cutting out the retaining frame.

any saw tearout. It is a good idea to use a fairly stiff brush to remove the sawdust from around the cut edges of the workpiece (see page 8). The sawdust tends to cling to the tight curves and can be a considerable nuisance when it comes to painting the piece.

6 Cut out the retaining frame from either 3mm (⅛in) MDF or 3mm (⅛in) plywood. Again, make the internal cut first.

7 Cut the securing panel. The external dimensions of the panel are the same as the external dimensions of the retaining frame. If your mirror is thinner than the 3mm (⅛in) material used, you can insert a piece of card between the back of the mirror and the panel to take up any slack.

8 Mark and drill clearance holes for the No. 2 woodscrews in the securing panel in the places marked on the template. Countersink the holes on the back of the securing panel. Drill pilot holes in the retaining frame, as shown on the template. At this stage, you can also mark and drill pilot holes in the back of the securing panel for the screw eyes.

9 Clean up as necessary. Glue the retaining frame in place on the back of the overlay with wood glue. Check the position of the frame carefully before committing the parts to the adhesive.

10 Decorate the project before you insert the mirror into its frame and assemble the back panel. Decorating at this point will avoid getting any splashes of paint or varnish on the mirror itself, which might well be difficult to clean off afterwards, because of the intricate lines of the overlay.

I used an antiquing kit to finish my frame. These kits, and other finishes, are obtainable from any good craft store. You may wish to colour your mirror to suit a room decor, or paint the butterflies and

oak leaves in natural colours, or even use a wood stain, with or without varnish depending on the effect you want. If you intend painting the project, it is a good idea to apply a coat of acrylic white primer or sealer before painting as MDF tends to soak up paint, particularly around the cut edges.

▲ Drilling the fixing holes in the retaining frame and securing sheet.

▼ The overlay, with the retaining frame glued in position, ready to be decorated.

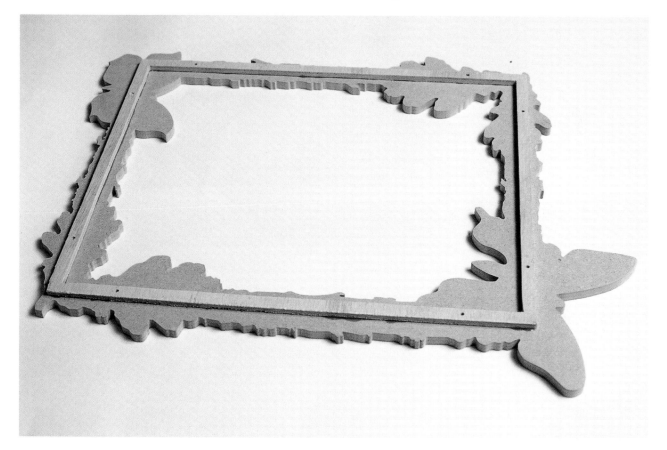

11 Once you have completed the decoration to your satisfaction, insert the mirror, pack with a sheet of card to ensure a good fit (if necessary), and screw in the woodscrews. All that remains is to screw in the eyes and fit the picture wire to hang your mirror.

▲ The completed mirror ready to have its eye hooks and picture wire fitted.

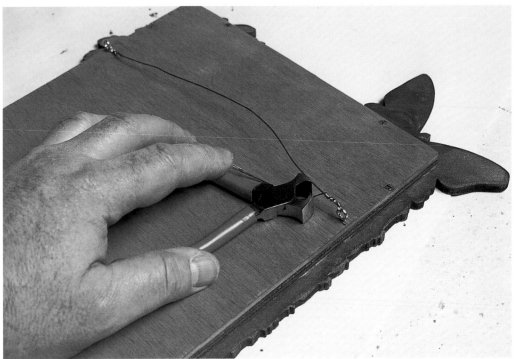

▲ Trimming the picture wire to length with a small pair of wire cutters.

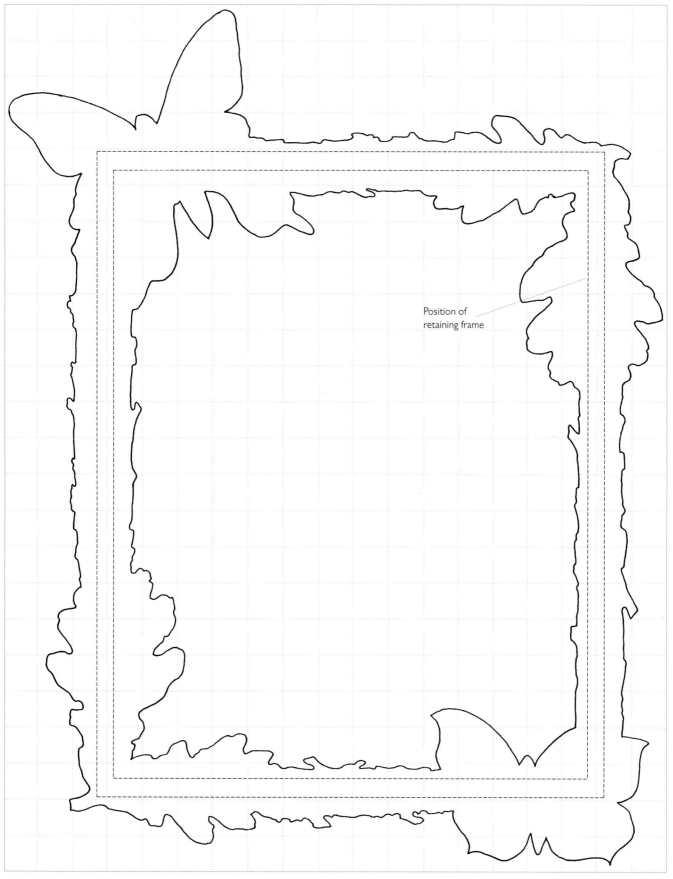

Position of
retaining frame

Mirror overlay

This template needs to be enlarged by 156%
1 square = 1.5 cm

Securing panel

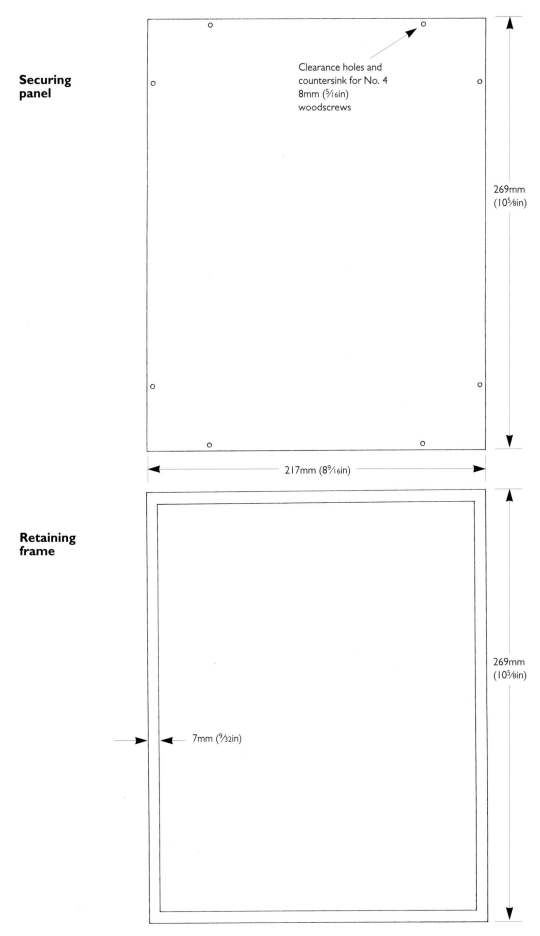

Clearance holes and
countersink for No. 4
8mm ($^5/_{16}$in)
woodscrews

269mm
(10$^5/_8$in)

217mm (8$^9/_{16}$in)

Retaining frame

269mm
(10$^5/_8$in)

7mm ($^9/_{32}$in)

Love spoon

The traditional Celtic love spoon is a popular subject for the scrollsaw, even though a lot of finishing has to be done after the scrollsawing is completed. The originals, of course, were created with nothing more than a penknife and many hours of whittling in the fields while tending the flocks. A young man would carve an intricate love spoon to impress his lady love with his undying devotion.

Each feature of the traditional spoon had a specific significance. The heart shapes on the design for this project need no explanation. The Celtic knotwork, intertwining loops of rope in the centre of the design, signify eternal togetherness. The spoon bowl indicated a willingness to provide for the bride.

The fairly straightforward design presented here is still, by the time you have completed it, a true labour of love. Patience is the particular virtue required for this project. The completed spoon will take around four or five hours of work to complete.

EQUIPMENT AND MATERIALS

- A piece of oak, or similar hard wood, around 300mm (11¾in) in length, 60mm (2⅜in) in width and around 12mm-20mm (½in-¾in) thick
- A craft knife
- A 3mm (⅛in) drill bit to make a hanging hole for a nail, and the starter holes for the internal cuts.
- Wood stain and polish to finish
- Spray mount

SCROLLSAW BLADE	**TEMPLATE**	
No. 5 or No. 7 general purpose scrollsaw blade	Love spoon	36

1 Make sure the grain of the wood you are using runs along the length of the spoon. This will ensure that the completed piece is strong. Do any surface preparation which may be required. If the surface is rough, then sand it as smooth as you can on both sides.

With most scrollsaw projects, it is much easier to carry out any surface preparation that is needed before committing the wood to the saw.

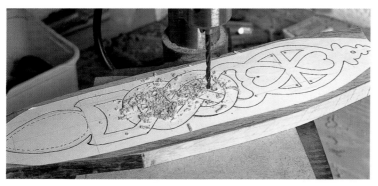

▲ Making the starter holes for the saw blade. The nail hole for hanging the completed love spoon is also drilled at this stage.

► The scrollsaw set up to make the internal cutout with the tension checked and the hold down device set up for the thickness of wood in use.

2 When you are happy with the surface of the wooden blank, prepare a cutting pattern on paper and glue it to the blank using spray mount. Once this is accomplished, mark out and drill all the starter holes, as well as the nail hole. The positions for these are shown on the template.

3 Make all the internal cutouts, making sure the blade tension and the hold down device are set correctly. Take your time at this stage – a degree of accuracy is essential if the finished love spoon is to look its best. Keep good control of the workpiece when changing from cutting across the grain to along the grain and back again. Remember that the saw will cut much faster across the grain of the wood than it will along the length of the grain.

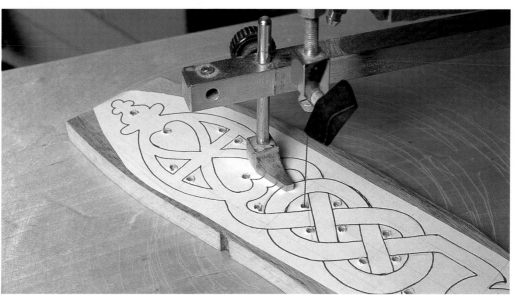

4 Once you have satisfactorily completed all the internal cutouts, set up the saw to make the external cut. Again, try to make the cut as accurate as you possibly can, following the cutting pattern lines exactly.

5 When you have completed the external cut, remove the remains of the cutting pattern and clean away any saw tearout with a little light sanding. Refer to the template, which shows where shaping is required. Using a craft knife, begin by cutting lightly across each line where the 'rope' passes underneath or over its crossing partner. You can then begin rounding and shaping the 'rope'.

6 Once you have finished carving, sand over your work with a strip of sandpaper. An emery board, used for filing nails, is useful for this job as it is flexible enough to cope with the rounded bends in the 'rope', and small enough to fit into the corners. You may need to do some more shaping with the craft knife.

7 The remaining section which needs your attention is the spoon bowl. I rounded the back of the example shown with a belt sander, but a rasp or any other coarse file will take away most of the waste material fairly quickly. The rounded underside can then be finished off with some sandpaper.

If you have a craft knife set, then use the large gouge to rough out most of the wood from the bowl of the spoon. Otherwise, use whatever you have to hand to accomplish this task. As a last resort, the job can be done with a piece of coarse sandpaper, but it will take longer. Once you feel you have taken out enough

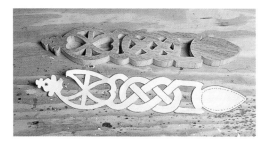

◄ The completed love spoon blank with the cutting pattern retained as a reference pattern for carving out the intertwining rope section of the spoon.

◄ Beginning to carve out the ropes of the intertwining rope section of the love spoon.

wood from the bowl of the spoon, sand it off to leave a nice smooth finish.

8 Depending on the type of wood you used – I used an oak offcut from a scrap drawer front – choose an appropriate finish. In the example shown, a light coat of Jacobean Oak varnish was used to give a deep colour. I only used one coat, to keep the end result from being too dark, and finished the project off with some wax polish.

▼ The spoon clamped to the bench while the gouge removes most of the material from the inside of the bowl of the spoon.

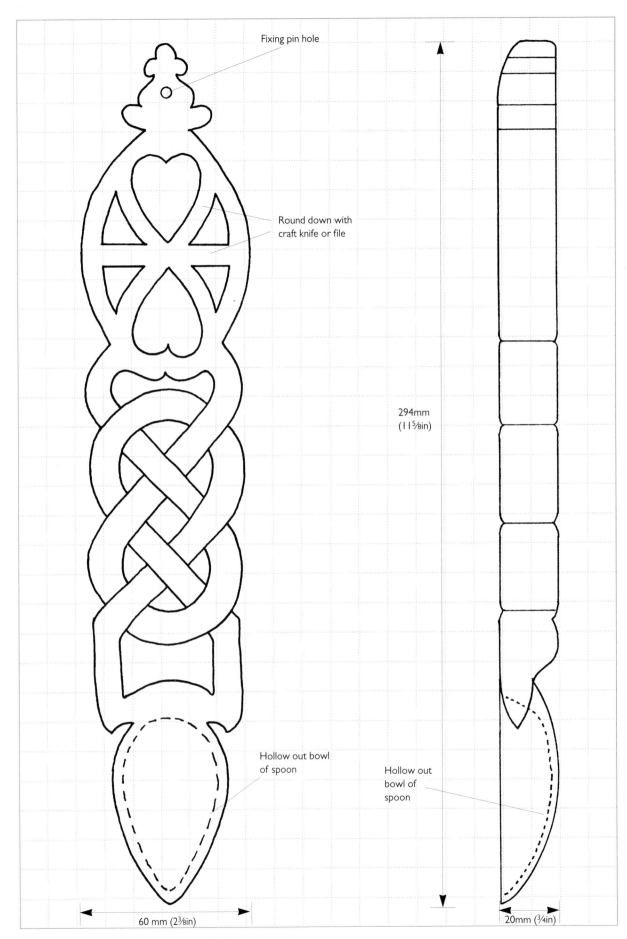

Fixing pin hole

Round down with
craft knife or file

294mm
(11⁵⁄₈in)

Hollow out bowl
of spoon

Hollow out
bowl of
spoon

60 mm (2³⁄₈in)

20mm (³⁄₄in)

This template needs to be enlarged by 128%
1 square = 1 cm

Plant pot screen

This project is designed to provide an attractive alternative to a plastic flower pot and saucer. The design shown in the template can easily be enlarged or reduced to suit whatever size pot you wish to hide and can easily be stack sawn to make a matching set. The ornamental cutout in each side of the plant pot screen allows the spout of a watering can to be poked in to add water to the plant's saucer. There are two wider areas in the internal cutout design. This permits watering at two different levels to suit a variety of saucer types – some are taller than others.

The sides of the project slot together for assembly. Two sides have a slot the thickness of the material – 6mm (¼in) in the example – cut down from the top of the side panels, while the other sides have a corresponding slot cut up from the bottom of each panel. The base is simply a square, of the same material as the sides, with a set of four rubber, self-adhesive, non-slip feet stuck on underneath to prevent the whole thing from sliding about on polished surfaces.

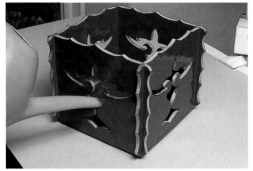

► The cutout design allows access to the plant pot with a watering can.

EQUIPMENT AND MATERIALS

- 4 pieces of 6mm (¼in) MDF (or your own choice), measuring 160mm x 203mm (6¼in x 8in)
- 1 piece of 6mm (¼in) MDF, measuring 180mm x 180mm (7in x 7in)
- 8 brass panel pins
- Wood glue

- Decorating materials of your choice. I used red and gold Humbrol enamel paints over a base coat of white acrylic primer
- 4 self-adhesive rubber feet (available from most hardware stores, or electronics suppliers)
- Double-sided adhesive tape
- Spray mount

SCROLLSAW BLADE

No. 7 skip-tooth scrollsaw blade

TEMPLATES

Side panel A	41
Side panel B	42
Base	43

1 Make up cutting patterns for side panels A and B, scaling them up or down to the size you want. A cutting pattern is not really necessary for the base as you can simply mark around the four assembled sides later on. Make each pair of MDF blanks into a stack using a few pieces of double-sided adhesive tape. Stick the patterns in place on top of the stacks with a little spray mount.

▼ Drilling the starter holes for the No. 7 skip-tooth blade, placing the starter hole so that the cut will begin and end on a sharp point in the design.

2 Mark and drill starter holes for the internal cutouts in the side panels. Set up your saw with a No. 7 skip-tooth blade and begin making the internal cutouts. The pieces from the internal cutouts can be adapted into gingerbread (see page 97) as they will be an attractive shape.

3 When you have completed the internal cutouts on both pairs of side panel blanks make the external cuts. Be careful when you cut round the slots

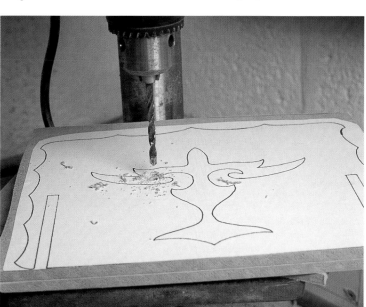

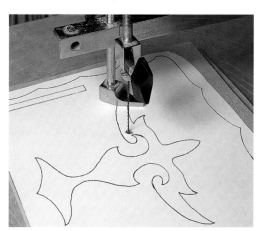

▲ The scrollsaw set up ready to begin the internal cutouts on the side panels.

◀ Taking extra care not to place too much stress on the slots as they are cut out.

▼ Using thick elastic bands as clamps to hold the slots tightly together while the glue sets.

as there will be very little strength in this area, so they can easily break off.

4 Once you have completed the cuts on both pairs of side panels, clean the pieces up carefully with a little sandpaper and check that they fit before you glue the pieces together. Do not try to force the slots together if they are a little tight, but carefully widen each slot a little at a time, with either a flat file or sandpaper, checking frequently for fit. It is often tempting to take away too much material at once. This can lead to a sloppy fit, making it difficult to keep the structure square.

5 Once you are happy with the fit of the four side panels, add wood glue along the inside edges of all the slots and fix them together. It is helpful if you can stand the assembled piece on a very flat surface to check that the bottom is perfectly even. Once you have assembled

the pieces, use a small set square to check that the internal angles are right angles before the glue sets. I used rubber bands to keep the structure together whilst the glue was drying.

6 When the glue has set, you will have a set of box-shaped side panels. Lay the structure over a piece of MDF material and mark an outline for the base by drawing around the outside with a sharp pencil. Cut this piece out with the scrollsaw and sand off any saw tearout.

▼ Drilling the pilot holes for the brass panel pins with a mini drill.

7 Make sure the base is a good fit, sanding level if necessary. Make a couple of pilot holes for the brass panel pins along each edge of the base, 3mm (⅛in) in from the edge. Select a drill bit which is slightly thinner than the panel pins and make the starter holes. Once you have drilled the starter holes in the base, use the base as a guide and drill corresponding holes through the side panels.

8 Glue the base in place. Use a nail punch to tap the panel pins in just below the surface of the base panel. Leave the completed plant pot screen to one side while the glue sets thoroughly.

9 Decorate the screen with a finish of your choice. Once all the paint, varnish or whatever you used has dried thoroughly, turn the unit over and attach the feet.

▲ Fitting the rubber self-adhesive feet to the base of the decorated plant pot screen.

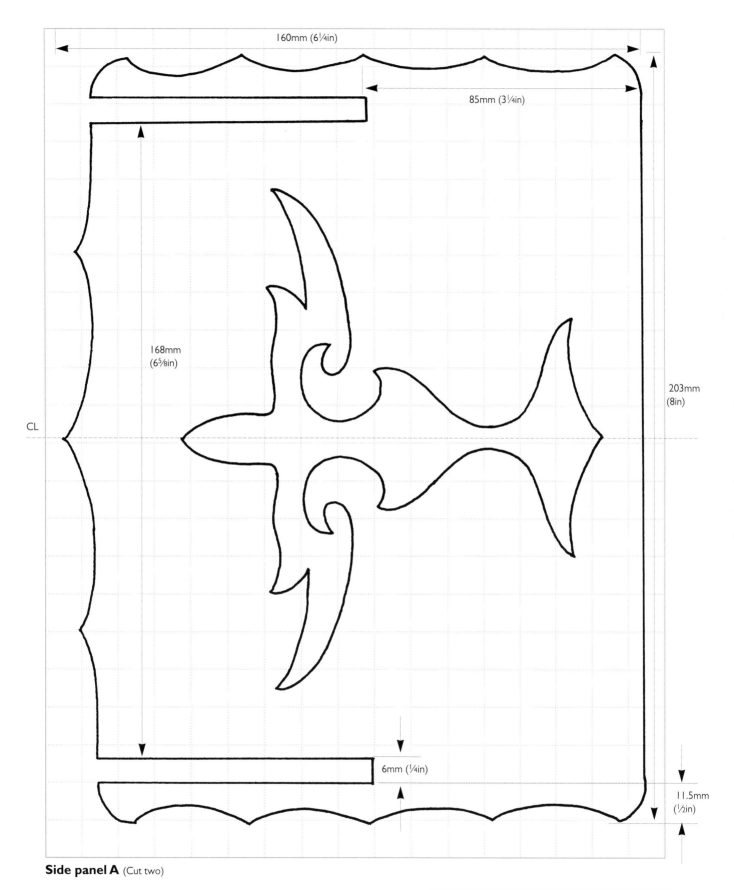

160mm (6¼in)

85mm (3¼in)

168mm
(6⅝in)

203mm
(8in)

CL

6mm (¼in)

11.5mm
(½in)

Side panel A (Cut two)

This template is actual size
1 square = 1cm

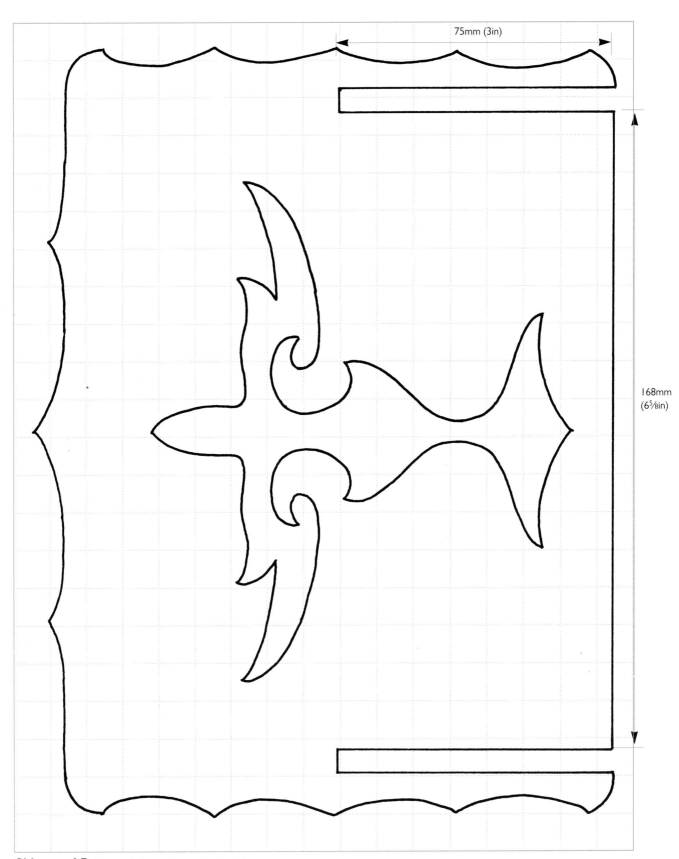

75mm (3in)

168mm
(6⅝in)

Side panel B (Cut two)   Dimensions as for Panel A

This template is actual size
I square = Icm

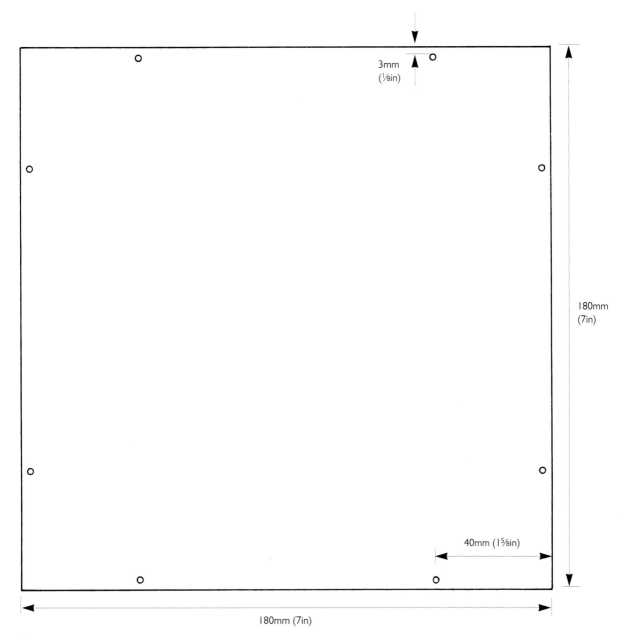

3mm
(⅛in)

180mm
(7in)

40mm (1⅝in)

180mm (7in)

Base

43

Scrollwork shelf

This project is a departure from the more usual forms of scrollwork shelf because it can be fitted to a wall at an angle of 45 degrees. The advantage of this arrangement is that the entire shelf unit with its two shelves, two shelf brackets and back panel can be cut from just one strip of wood measuring 755mm x 125mm (29¾in x 5in). Although the design is intricate, there are no internal cutouts to make.

You can also adapt this design to make a pair of opposing shelves, as I have done, by reversing one back panel. You will need double the quantities of material. The instructions outline the procedure for one shelf and detail any variations needed for the double unit as appropriate. There is a separate template provided to make the brackets for the pair of opposing shelves.

EQUIPMENT AND MATERIALS

- A piece of wood, MDF or plywood, 755mm x 125mm (29¾in x 5in) and 6mm (¼in) thick
- 2 mirror screws with caps of your choice
- 8 woodscrews No. 4 15mm (⅝in), to fix the shelves and brackets
- Drill bits, to drill clearance holes for the mirror screws and pilot and clearance holes for the woodscrews, see chart on page 8

- Wood glue
- Double-sided adhesive tape, if you intend to make an opposing pair of shelves
- Paint, undercoat or whatever else you decide on as suitable decoration for the finished project
- Spray mount

SCROLLSAW BLADE

You will need to choose a suitable scrollsaw blade for the material you have chosen (see page 8 for details). For MDF (used in the examples shown) you will need a No. 7 skip-tooth blade. A slightly finer blade will work well, but a coarser blade may struggle with the tight turns involved in the design.

TEMPLATES

Shelf	49
Bracket	49
Back panel	49
Pair of opposing shelves	50

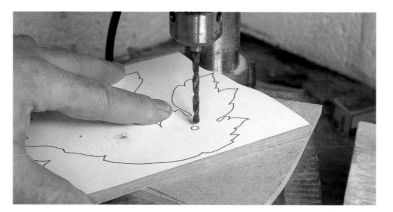

▲ Using the larger drill bit to make the holes for the mounting screws.

◄ Countersinking the holes prior to cutting out the panel.

▲ Sawing blanks using the pattern as a rough guide.

1 Make up a full-sized cutting pattern using the templates. You can make the design larger or smaller by scaling the pattern up or down. Lay the cutting pattern on the sheet material and check that it fits adequately. Once you are satisfied with the position of the pattern, attach it to the blank with spray mount. If you are making one shelf, you can then cut roughly around the shapes.

Opposing shelves Cut out blanks for the back panel pieces, shelves and brackets. Attach the blanks firmly together with double-sided adhesive tape in strategic areas on the waste side of the cutting line. Stack up the four shelves under one cutting pattern ready for sawing and the same for the four brackets. The two back panels can then be stack sawn. The maximum stack thickness will only be

about 24mm (approximately 1in) and should be within the capabilities of most scrollsaws, although it will take slightly longer to cut them out. You will only make three cuts to make in order to produce all the component parts for the opposing shelves.

2 Drill the clearance holes for the shelf and bracket fixing woodscrews, which are marked 'B' on the template, and the clearance holes for the mirror screws, marked 'A' on the template. Before you countersink these holes, you will need to decide which way you want your shelf to lean when it is in position.

▼ Cutting the back panel using the scrollsaw. Note the cut begins and finishes at a sharp point. The waste material is cut away in sections to allow a sharper finish to the leaves.

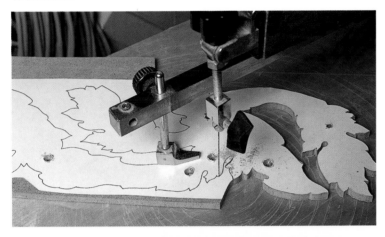

► Sanding away the small amount of saw tearout from the back panel.

► Marking the positions for the pilot holes for the shelf fixing screws.

This will determine which side of the panel each hole is countersunk. Each set of holes will need to be countersunk from opposite sides. Countersink the shelf and bracket fixing holes from the back of the panel and countersink the mirror screw holes from the front of the panel.

3 Set up the saw with an appropriate blade for the material you are using. Make sure the hold down device is set and carefully cut around the lines on the cutting patterns. Start each cut at a sharp angle on the design (there are plenty to choose from but select one near the edge of the material for ease) and simply follow the pattern round until the cut is completed. This done you will be able to stack saw the two shelves and brackets.

If your saw has a limited throat capacity you may find some difficulty in accommodating the length of the back panel. Fit a fine-grade spiral blade (see page 7 for more details). You will then be able to work the panel across the saw table without turning the panel at all. Using this method you should be able to manage with a saw that has a throat capacity of about 150mm (6in).

4 Once you have completed the cutting, clean up any saw tearout with a piece of sandpaper. It is also a good idea to clean off any sawdust from the cutting lines with a small stiff brush (see page 8).

◀ Using a mini drill to make the pilot holes for the shelf fixing screws.

▼ Tightening the screws to fix the shelf in position.

5 Begin the assembly of the shelves. Place one shelf on the back panel. Check that the edge at the back of the shelf is straight with a steel ruler. Mark out and drill pilot holes in the shelf.

6 Fit the shelf by adding a line of wood glue along the rear edge of the shelf. Then attach the shelf in the position marked on the back panel and tighten the fixing screws.

7 You will now be able to obtain an accurate position for the bracket, which should be centred underneath the shelf. Mark the positions for the pilot holes in the brackets and drill them. Attach the bracket with a smear of wood glue along the back and top edges and screw it into place. Repeat this procedure for the remaining shelf (or shelves if you are making **opposing shelves**).

If there is a gap between the top of the bracket and the underside of the shelf, clamp the two together while the glue sets. You can use a clamp if you have a suitable one, or a few elastic bands will do

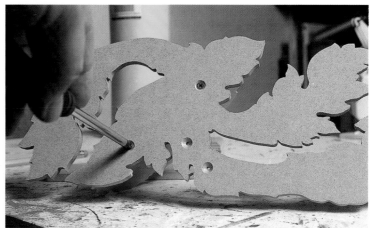

▲ Marking the positions of pilot holes in the bracket using the shelf as a reference.

47

► A complete shelf unit with rubber band 'clamps' in place.

the trick. Another advantage of having an intricate design is that there are plenty of places for elastic bands to hold on to.

8 Once the glue has set, your completed shelf unit is ready for decoration. The shelf units shown were made from MDF material, so a coat of white acrylic primer was applied before painting. This coat was lightly sanded down to a smooth finish when it dried and a coat of coloured paint applied. The front of the unit was painted first and

allowed to dry. The edges needed a second coat, because the cut material was more absorbent. When dry, a further coat may well be required to obtain a good finish. Once all the paint is fully dried, you may wish to apply a coat of gloss or satin varnish to give the shelves a sheen.

9 When mounting your shelf units, use a spirit level along one of the shelves to make certain that you are fixing it at the correct angle, or your ornaments may well slide off on to the floor.

► The finished item ready for decoration

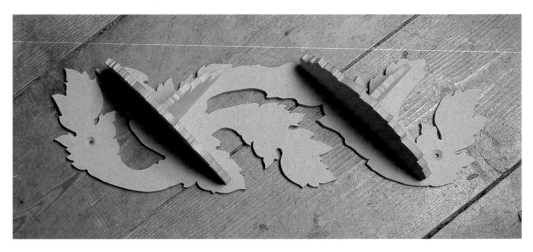

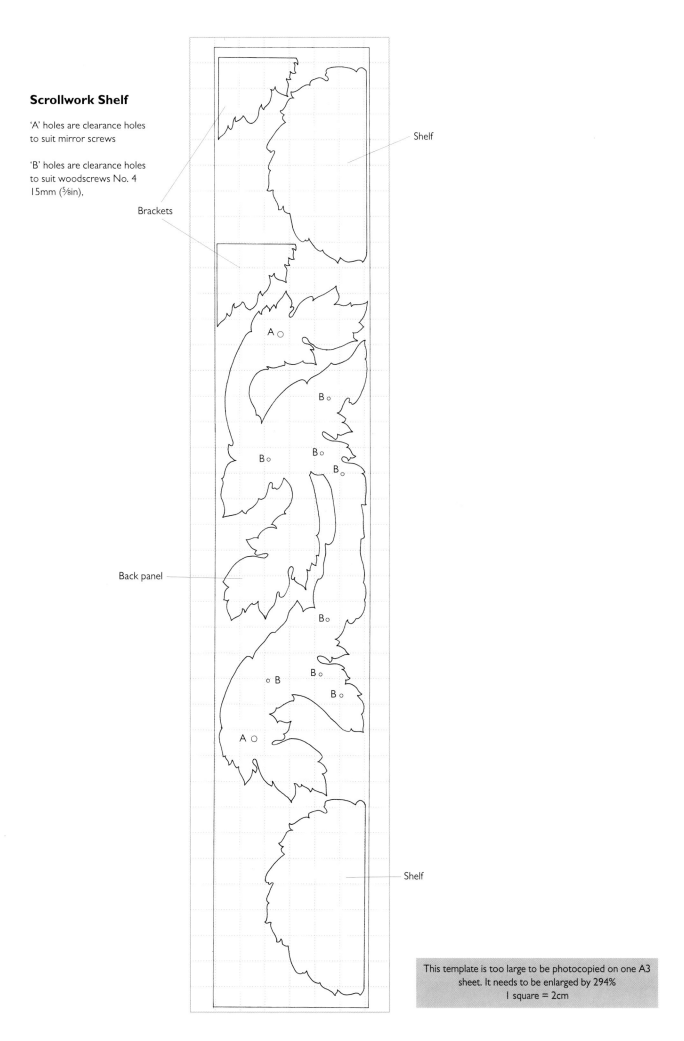

Scrollwork Shelf

'A' holes are clearance holes
to suit mirror screws

'B' holes are clearance holes
to suit woodscrews No. 4
15mm (⅝in),

Brackets

Shelf

A ○

B ○

B ○   B ○

B ○

Back panel

B ○

B ○

○ B   B ○

A ○

Shelf

This template is too large to be photocopied on one A3
sheet. It needs to be enlarged by 294%
1 square = 2cm

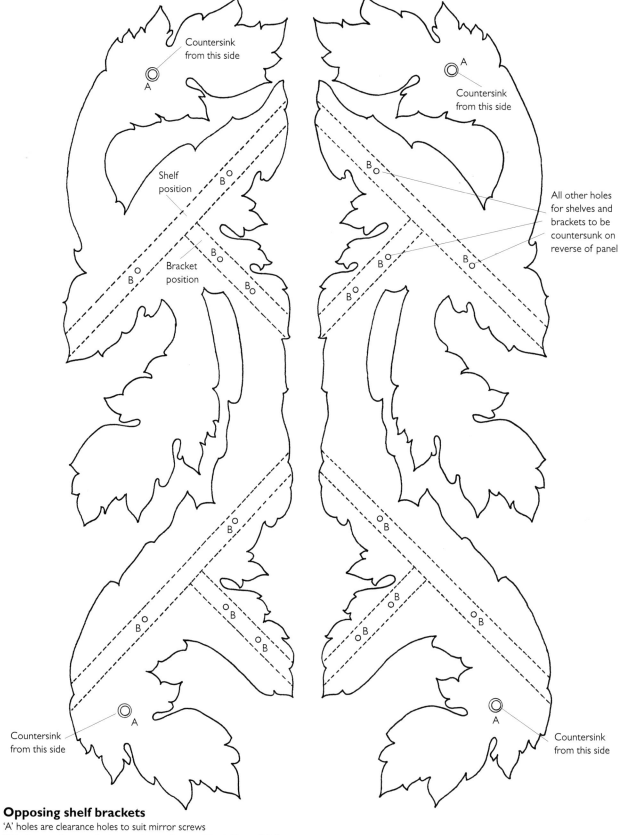

Countersink
from this side

A

Shelf
position

B

Bracket
position

B

B

B

Countersink
from this side

A

A

Countersink
from this side

B

All other holes
for shelves and
brackets to be
countersunk on
reverse of panel

B

B

B

B

B

B

B

B

A

Countersink
from this side

Opposing shelf brackets
'A' holes are clearance holes to suit mirror screws
'B' holes are clearance holes to suit woodscrews No. 4 15mm (⅝in)

Mug tree

This handy little item makes a good starter project. It has practical design features, but it is fairly undemanding to make. A degree of accuracy is needed when cutting the pieces where the two halves of the tree join and, of course, the base needs to be flat.

The example shown here was made from two pieces of pine board measuring 280mm x 200mm (11in x 7⅞in) and 280mm x 160mm (11in x 6¼in). These could easily be salvaged from an old item of furniture or made up from a piece of pine board, just as this one was. The thickness of the wood I used was 17mm (¹¹⁄₁₆in). Other thicknesses of wood or sheet material can just as easily be used, but remember to adjust the slots shown on the template where the two parts join.

EQUIPMENT AND MATERIALS

Pine board, or your choice of material
- 1 piece, 280mm x 200mm (11in x 7⅞in)
- 1 piece, 280mm x 160mm (11in x 6¼in)

Pieces a little larger than these dimensions will make handling easier.

- Flat drill bit, to cut out the hole in the ring at the top of the tree (This can be cut with your scrollsaw if you don't have large flat drill bits.)
- Wood glue
- Paint or lacquer to decorate the piece
- Spray mount

▲ Using spray mount to fix the cutting patterns in place on the blanks.

1 Make up a cutting pattern for both pieces. If you are using a different thickness of material than that suggested, make the necessary adjustments to the dimensions of the slots where the two pieces fit together. Stick the patterns in place with spray mount.

2 Decide whether you intend to drill or cut out the ring. If you intend to cut it out, drill a starter hole for the saw

▶ Making the hole in the top of one half of the mug tree with a flat drill bit.

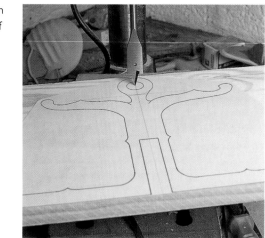

blade and make an internal cutout. If you intend to drill the hole, use the flat drill bit suggested.

3 Begin cutting each piece at the base of the tree leg. This part of the pattern provides a sharp angle, which will help to avoid any slight inaccuracy between the start and finish of the cut. The base of the legs should be flat. Check this after you have finished cutting with a straight edge such as a steel rule.

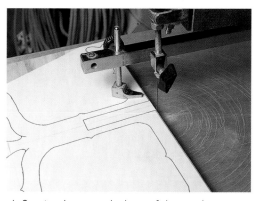

▲ Starting the cut at the base of the tree leg.

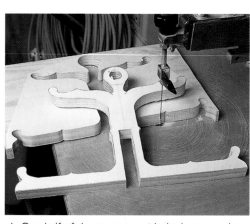

▲ One half of the mug tree with the bottom edge checked for flatness.

4 Sand off any saw tearout from the sides and edges of the pieces. Slot the cutout piece into the waste part of the blank then sand the sides. This will help to support the fragile parts of the piece.

5 When you have cut out both pieces of the design, check that they slot easily together. Do not push too hard if the fit is a little too tight or you will snap off the sides, which are rather brittle at this stage and only gain full strength once they have been glued together. File or sand as needed to make the two pieces slide together easily, creating a good close fit. Don't be tempted to remove too much material or you will have to start again.

6 Add a little wood glue to the inner surfaces of both parts and slide them together to form the mug tree. A little light clamping pressure can be applied if you have clamps to hand, otherwise bind the pieces tightly together with some elastic bands until the glue has completely set.

7 Once the glue has set, remove the clamping arrangement and clean up as necessary. Check that the base is level on a flat surface and sand if necessary.

8 Decorate the mug tree. The example was given an undercoat of white acrylic primer, rubbed down lightly and then given two coats of bright orange Humbrol enamel.

▲ Using the waste part of the blank to support the fragile parts of the piece during sanding.

◄ The glued together mug tree awaiting decoration.

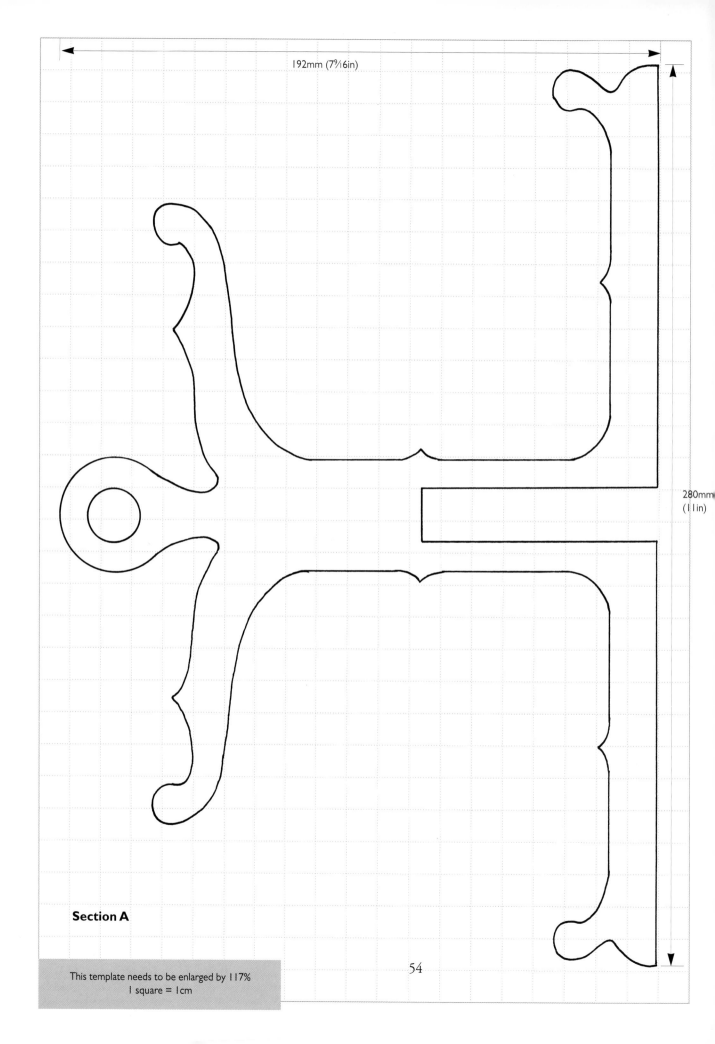

192mm (7⁹⁄₁₆in)

280mm (11in)

Section A

54

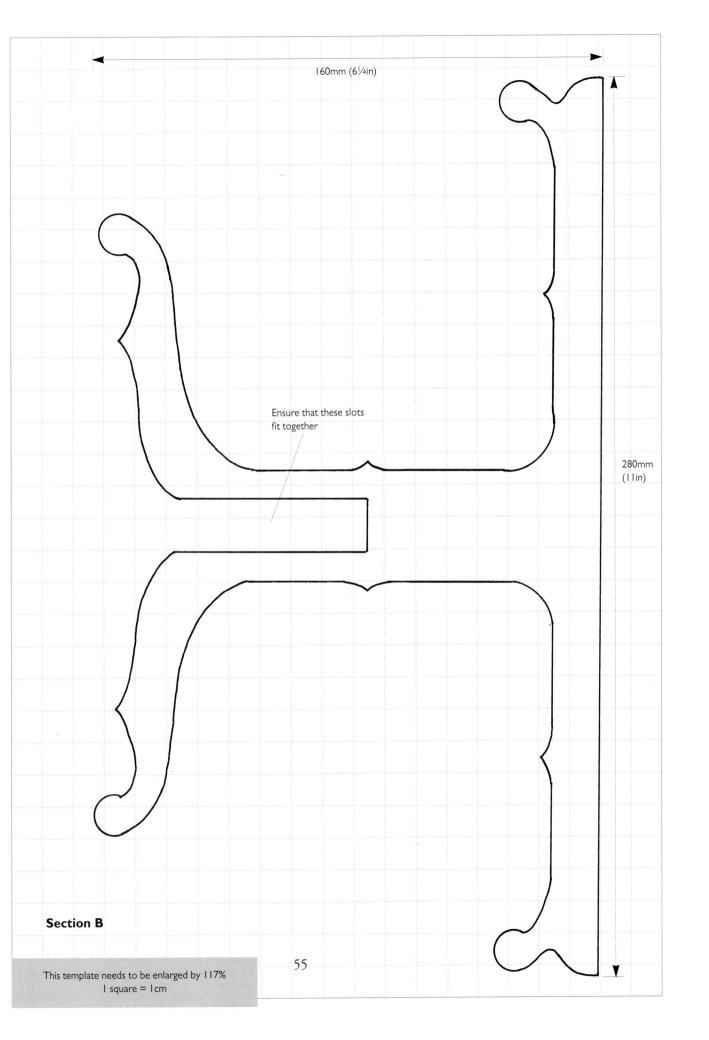

160mm (6¼in)

Ensure that these slots
fit together

280mm
(11in)

Section B

This template needs to be enlarged by 117%
1 square = 1cm

Heraldic shield house numbers

H ere is a straightforward project which will brighten up the outside of your house. The project should present no special difficulties and can be easily decorated in the style and colour of your choice. There are a couple of different shield shapes for you to choose from.

The numerals provided are based on a medieval design from the early fourteenth century, so are in keeping with the flavour of the project. The advantage of making numerals with the scrollsaw is the fact that you can easily make them to any finished size you want.

EQUIPMENT AND MATERIALS

Sheet material suitable for outdoor conditions, 6mm (¼in) thick marine plywood is ideal, MDF or normal grade plywood finished with yacht varnish are cheaper options. The amount of material needed:

- Shield, approximately 200mm x 155mm (7⅞in x 6⅛in)

- Numerals, approximately an A4 sheet, 297mm x 210 mm (11¹¹⁄₁₆in x 8¼in)
- Adhesive, such as epoxy resin
- Paints and varnish for decoration
- 2 mirror screws with brass caps (or silver if you prefer), to mount the completed project
- Drill bits, for clearance holes for the mirror screws, see chart on page 8

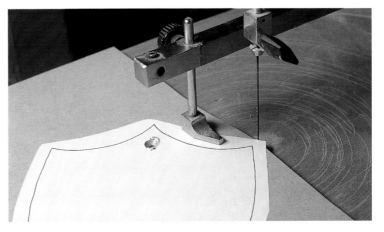

1 Make a cutting pattern of the shield you prefer. The sizes of the originals shown here are 190mm x 144mm (7½in x 5¾in) and 185mm x 154mm (7¼in x 6⅛in) but you can, of course, make them whatever size you wish by scaling the template up or down. Remember to scale the numerals you are going to use by the same amount. Once you are happy with your cutting pattern, stick it onto the sheet material blank with spray mount. If you intend cutting more than one shield at once you will need to stack saw the identical pieces (see page 16).

When stack sawing, place the double-sided adhesive tape in the waste areas of the blank. Once the cut has been completed, the pieces will easily separate from each other. Otherwise the process of pulling the identical pieces apart, especially in the case of the numerals which, once cut out, will have very little mechanical strength, could cause breakage.

2 Set up the scrollsaw with the No. 7 skip-tooth blade and adjust the hold down device. Cut around the shield. Once the cut has been completed, remove the remains of the cutting pattern from the shield and gently sand away any saw tearout to leave a smooth finish ready for decoration.

3 Mark out and drill the clearance holes for the mirror screws. Once you have drilled out the screw holes, countersink them sufficiently to accommodate the mirror screws flush with the surface of the shield.

4 Copy the drawing of the numerals you are going to use in the size you want. In the example shown here, the numerals are a little under 80mm (3in). If you need more than one of the same numeral – number twenty-two for instance – stack saw the pieces.

▲ The scrollsaw set up with a No. 7 skip-tooth blade with the hold down device in position, ready to cut out the shield.

◀ Drilling the fixing holes for the mirror screws.

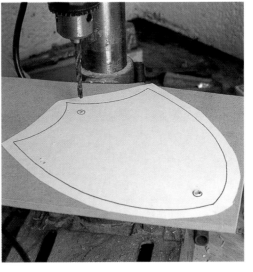

► Drilling starter holes for the internal cutouts on those numerals which require it.

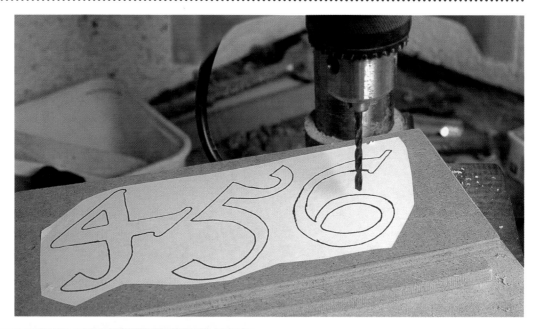

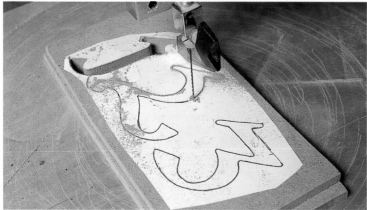

▲ Cutting out the numerals.

5 Drill starter holes and complete the internal cutouts first, if necessary. Make the external cuts to complete your numerals. Sand off any saw tearout as before.

6 Apply a coat of primer to both the shield and the numerals and leave it to dry. There is no need to paint the underside of the numerals as these will be glued to the shield a little later when all

► Shield and numerals ready for the decoration stage. The numerals have been undercoated with white acrylic primer.

the painting is complete. Once the primer is thoroughly dry, mark out the pattern you wish to use on the shield and paint on your colours. While the shield is drying, you can paint the numerals in whatever colour you want.

7 When the paint is completely dry, position and glue the numerals to the shield. I used fast-setting epoxy resin, which sets in about four minutes.

8 When the glue is dry, apply several coats of good quality yacht varnish to both the front and back of the shield to provide a weatherproof finish. It is best to coat the front, including the numerals, and the sides first and then set the shield aside on a tin or something similar to dry. You can then coat the back of the shield.

9 Once the shield is dry attach it to your chosen wall. Mark the fixing holes by pushing a pencil or ballpoint pen through the holes in the shield and then drill fixing holes. Insert wall plugs if you need to and fix the shield to the wall using the two mirror screws. This done, screw on the mirror screw caps.

▲ Gluing the numerals in place on the fully painted shields prior to varnishing and mounting.

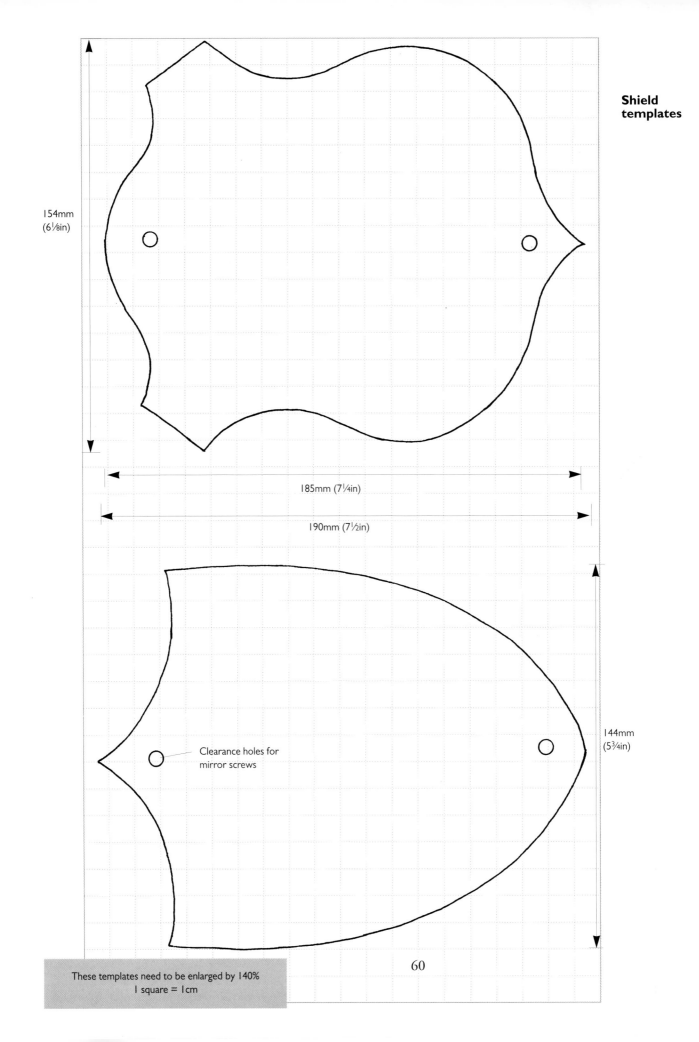

Shield templates

154mm
(6⅛in)

185mm (7¼in)

190mm (7½in)

144mm
(5¾in)

Clearance holes for
mirror screws

60

These templates need to be enlarged by 140%
1 square = 1cm

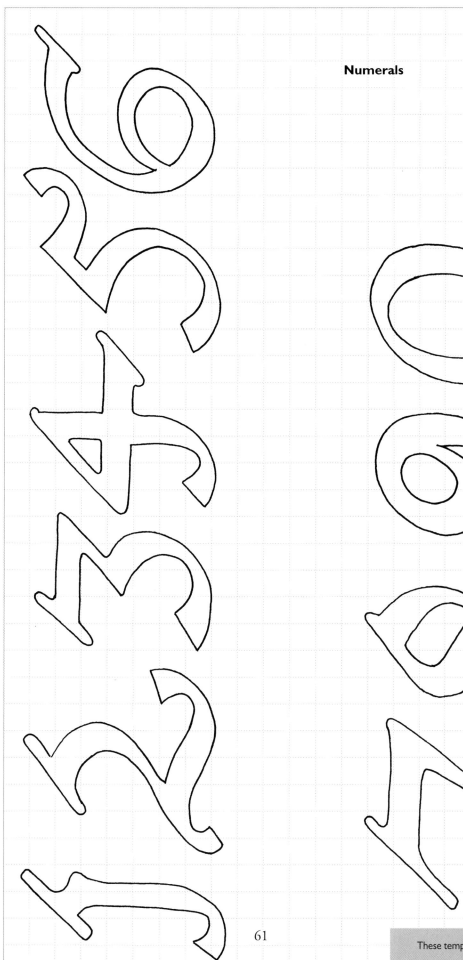

61

These templates need to be enlarged by 140%
1 square = 1cm

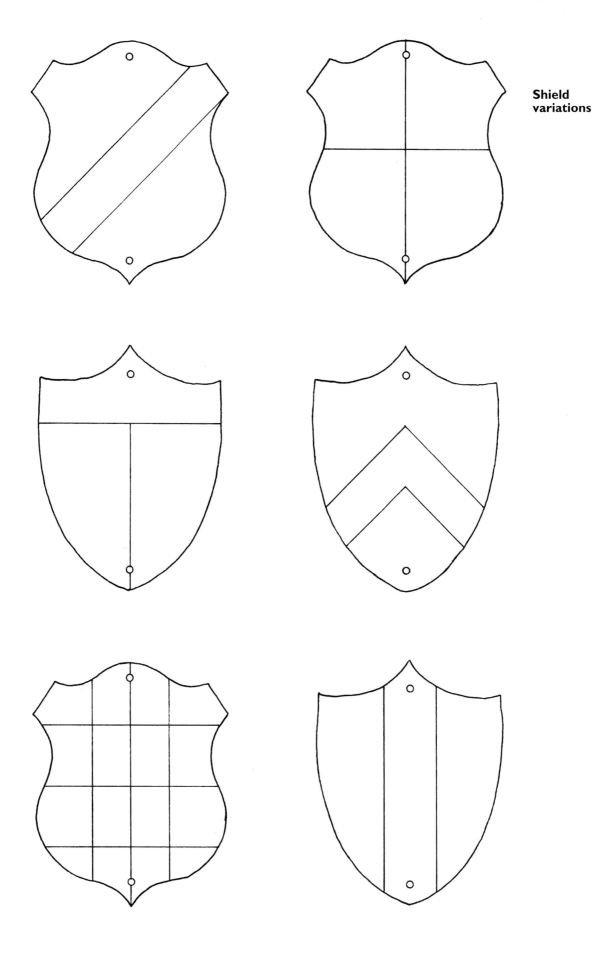

Shield variations

Collector's cabinet

This project is a little more involved than most of the others in the book, although it is not difficult to construct providing you approach it methodically, as outlined in the step-by-step instructions. The cabinet consists of a group of boxes which have a decorative rear and front panel. The box corners are trimmed with scroll-cut ramin wood. The example has mirrors at the back of the boxes to reflect the back of the object on display. The outside of the cabinet is decorated with antique and crackle paint effects finishes.

The front and back panels of the cabinet may be too large for some scrollsaws. If this is the case, use a spiral blade.

EQUIPMENT AND MATERIALS

MDF or plywood, 6mm (¼in) thick, in the following sizes:

- 2 pieces 320mm x 338mm (12⅝in x 13⁵⁄₁₆in)
- 5 pieces 126mm x 120mm (5in x 4¾in)
- 2 pieces 270mm x 120mm (10⅝in x 4¾in)
- 4 pieces right angle ramin section 120mm (4¾in) long
- 1 piece 138mm x 120mm (5⁷⁄₁₆in x 4¾in)
- 15mm (⁹⁄₁₆in) panel pins
- Wood glue
- Decorating materials of your choice
- Mirror card if you intend using this option

SCROLLSAW BLADE

No. 7 skip-tooth blade or a spiral blade
for smaller saws.

TEMPLATES

Decorative front and back panel	68
Box arrangement	69
Right angle moulding	68

▼ The scrollsaw set up with a skip-tooth blade inserted into one of the starter holes ready to make the internal cutouts. Note that only one of the panel blanks has internal cutouts.

1 Make up a cutting pattern for the front and back panels. Cut out two MDF blanks for the panels, and clean them up with sandpaper. Stick the cutting pattern in place on one of the blanks.

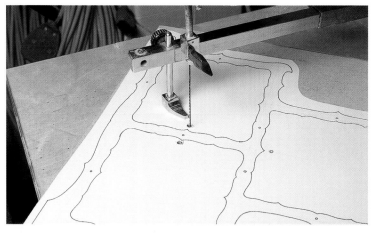

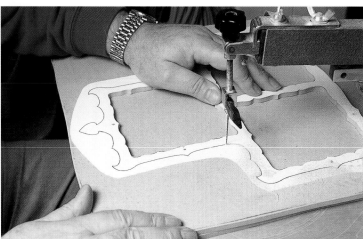

▲ Sawing round the external cutting line of the two panels.

2 Drill starter holes for the internal cutouts on the front panel. The rear panel does not have any cutouts. Set up the blank on the scrollsaw and make all three internal cutouts.

3 Take the front panel, with internal cutouts, and the as yet uncut back panel. Make a stack of the two pieces using double-sided adhesive tape. Use small pieces of tape and try to make sure the tape is outside the cutting line. Set up the stack of panels on your saw and make the external cut, which will ensure that both panels are precisely the same. Pay particular attention to the bottom of the panels, the feet of the cabinet, which need to be perfectly straight.

4 Decorate the back and front panels.

5 Cut out the rectangular pieces that make up the nest of boxes which fit between the front and back panels. The equipment and materials list has the exact

▲ Drilling through the pilot holes to get an accurate location for the nail holes in the adjoining piece.

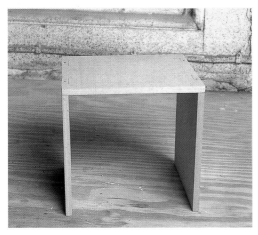

▲ The top section of the upper box completed.

◄ The main crosspiece and lower divider glued and pinned in position on the three-sided section completed in the last step.

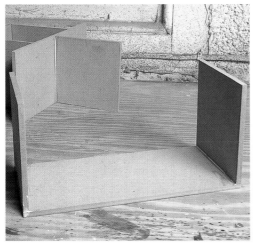

▲ The lower box section completed and ready to be joined onto the rest of the nest of boxes.

sizes you will need, but refer to the box arrangement templates if you have any doubts. You can cut these pieces on the scrollsaw, or any other way you wish as long as you end up with a pile of rectangles of the correct sizes.

6 Assemble the nest of boxes (see above). The panels are glued and pinned with panel pins to hold them together. The strength of the finished cabinet will be added to by the front and back panels and the reinforcing corners.

Make sure you assemble the box pieces at right angles. Check the angles with a set square. Use a small drill bit to make pilot holes for the panel pins, as this will prevent the MDF from splitting when you knock in the panel pins.

7 Decorate the inside of the boxes. Humbrol silver metallic paint was used on the example here. The metallic effect was chosen to match the mirror cards, which were attached to the back panel at a later stage.

▲ The completed nest of boxes ready to be joined onto the main panels.

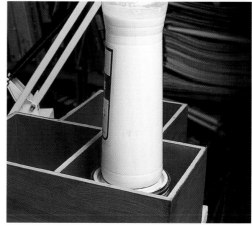

▲ *Above* Using a mini-drill to make the pilot holes for the panel pins in the back panel, using the pre-drilled holes in the back panel to ensure accurate alignment.

▶ *Above right* Using a large bottle of PVA glue as a weight to hold the mirror flat while the adhesive sets.

8 Once the paint has dried, decorate the outside of the nest of boxes. This step is best done before the final assembly is carried out so that no paint or other decorating materials will be spilt onto the front and back panels.

9 Fit the back panel to the nest of boxes with glue and panel pins. Make sure that the back panel aligns correctly with the nest of boxes, as there is little margin for error when placing the holes for the panel pins. When you are completely happy with the alignment,

make pilot holes for the panel pins to avoid splitting the MDF sheet. Apply a smear of glue to the back edge of the nest of boxes, attach the back panel and tap in the panel pins, making sure they fit close to the surface of the back panel. Use a nail, or pin punch if necessary, to avoid bruising the surface of the panel.

10 If you want to attach mirror card to the back of the boxes, fit it at this point. Check the internal measurements of the boxes, and mark out the relevant sizes on the back of the mirror card (this is usually a white plastic sheet which takes a pen or pencil marks easily). Use a craft knife with a sharp blade to cut the mirror card out and glue it in place. Use fast-setting epoxy adhesive, and weigh down the mirror card while the adhesive sets.

11 Fix the front panel in place, taking care with the location as you did for the back panel. Glue and pin as before and allow to set.

12 Make up a cutting pattern based on the right angle moulding template. Cut four pieces of moulding to length, checking them with dimensions

▲ Panel pins being tapped home with a light hammer after a smear of glue has been applied between the reverse of the front panel and the edges of the nest of boxes.

▲ The right angle moulding marked on both sides.

▲ Cutting the edge on the length of moulding. It is impractical to use the hold down device, so watch your fingers and work slowly.

on your cabinet. Lay your cutting pattern in place and mark out the cutting line with a marker pen. Do this on the inside and outside of each piece of moulding until you have marked all four pieces.

13 Set up the saw to cut out the decorative border trim. Make the cuts along the lines you have drawn and sand the edges down smooth. A slight tapering in at the edges will add to the effect.

14 Decorate the four trim pieces. The ones shown here were given a single coat of Humbrol metallic gold, straight onto the bare wood. When the paint has dried, glue the trims in place.

15 Check that the cabinet will stand perfectly level on a flat surface. It is at this point that you will discover if you have been sufficiently accurate when fitting the front and back panels. If the cabinet is wobbly, sand off the feet until it stands firm.

► Gluing the decorated and shaped right angle moulding with fast-setting epoxy resin.

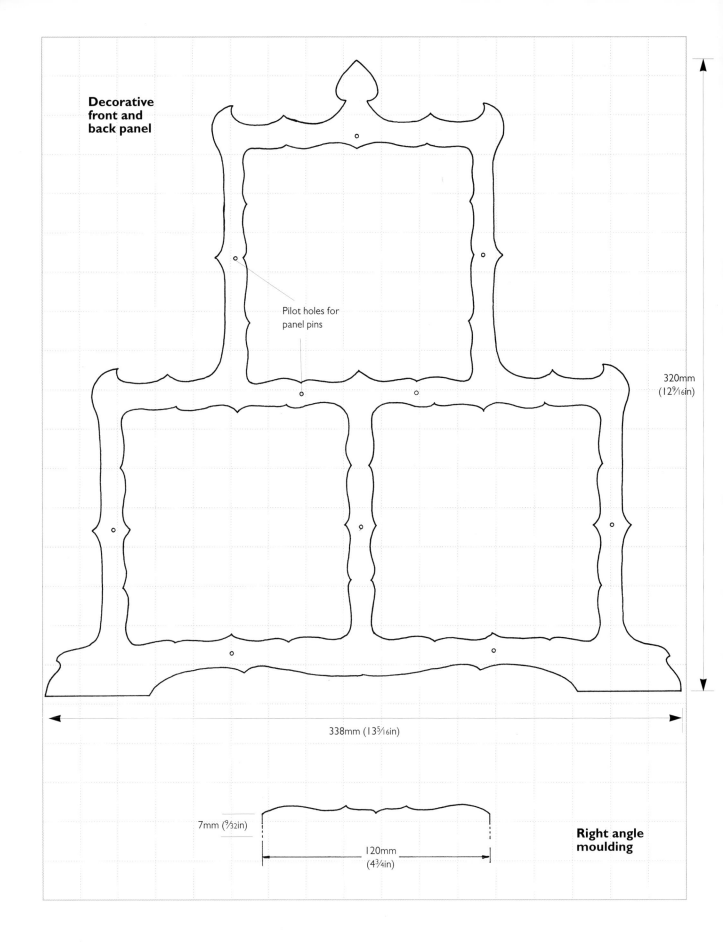

Decorative front and back panel

Pilot holes for panel pins

320mm (12⁹⁄₁₆in)

338mm (13⁵⁄₁₆in)

7mm (⁹⁄₃₂in)

120mm (4¾in)

Right angle moulding

This template is too large to be photocopied on one A3 sheet. It needs to be enlarged by 192% 1 square = 2cm

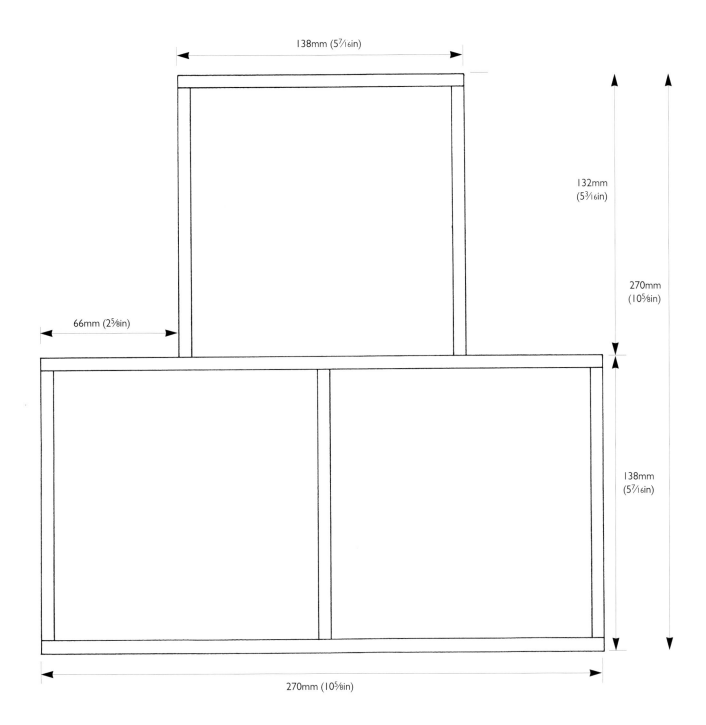

138mm (5⁷⁄₁₆in)

132mm (5³⁄₁₆in)

270mm (10⁵⁄₈in)

66mm (2⁵⁄₈in)

138mm (5⁷⁄₁₆in)

270mm (10⁵⁄₈in)

Box arrangement

69

Book ends

Not only is this project useful, it could also be an opportunity to use up some offcuts of wood. While the example shown was made from some 18mm (¾in) thick pine, it would have been preferable to use some hardwood, as this would have required less sanding after the cutting out had been completed.

The book ends are made from two parts: a face plate and a support bracket. This arrangement avoids the need for the book ends to be very heavy in order to prevent them falling over. The two parts, when cut out and sanded, are simply glued and screwed together to make the finished items. The project can then be decorated to match a room, or finished in whatever manner you prefer.

EQUIPMENT AND MATERIALS

- 2 pieces of wood of 150mm x 145mm (6in x 5¾in)
- 2 pieces of wood of 145mm x 75mm (5¾in x 3in) and about 18mm (2¾in) thick
- 4 wood screws to suit the thickness of the timber you are using
- Wood glue
- Decorating materials of your choice to finish the book ends

TEMPLATES

Faceplate	73
Support brackets	73

1 Make up a set of cutting patterns. Prepare two sets of blanks. Attach each pair of blanks together with double-sided adhesive tape. Stick the pattern in place in the top of the blanks and make the starter holes for the internal cutouts with a drill. If you are working with very thick material you may have to cut all four pieces separately.

2 Set up your scrollsaw to make the internal cutouts. Check the blade tension is correct and the hold down device is in place. Thread the blade through the first starter hole and make the cut. Continue until all the internal cutouts have been made. Notice that the pattern on the support bracket is a repeat of the pattern on the face plates, making the two separate parts look as if they belong together.

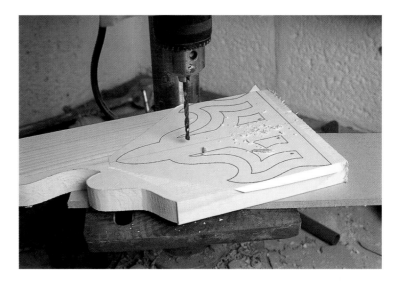

3 Make the external cuts until you have finished each piece. Clean up any saw tearout with sandpaper and, if needed, a small half-round file is handy for getting into the inside edge. This was essential on the pieces shown in the example because it was made from pine,

▲ Drilling the starter holes for the internal cutouts.

◄ The workpiece set up on the scrollsaw, making the internal cutouts.

► The book end parts with the fixing holes drilled and countersunk, ready for final assembly.

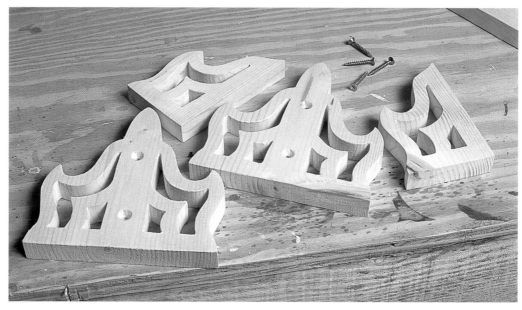

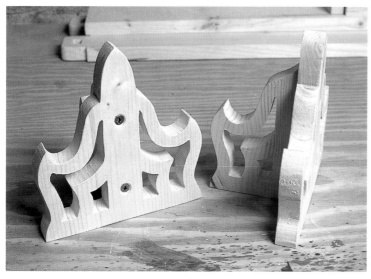

▲ The pair of book ends assembled ready for decoration.

which will join the face plate and bracket together. On a flat surface, put the bracket in place and mark out for two holes as shown on the template. Countersink the face plate holes from the opposite side to where the bracket is going. The countersink holes will be on the same side of the face plate as the books once the project has been finished, so make sure the countersink is deep enough for the head of the screw to sit slightly below the surface of the wood. This will stop the screw from scratching any of the books kept between the book ends.

which is an open grained wood so tends to fluff up when cut, giving a woolly finish.

4 Stand the two parts of each book end together on a flat surface, checking that the straight edges are true. Use a sanding block to correct matters if they are a little out of line. Mark the holes in the face plates for the woodscrews

5 Wipe a little wood glue along the flat side of each bracket where it will join onto the face plate, and press the brackets into place. Screw in the woodscrews, making sure that each screw sits properly in its countersink. Allow the glue to set thoroughly and then decorate to your own preferences.

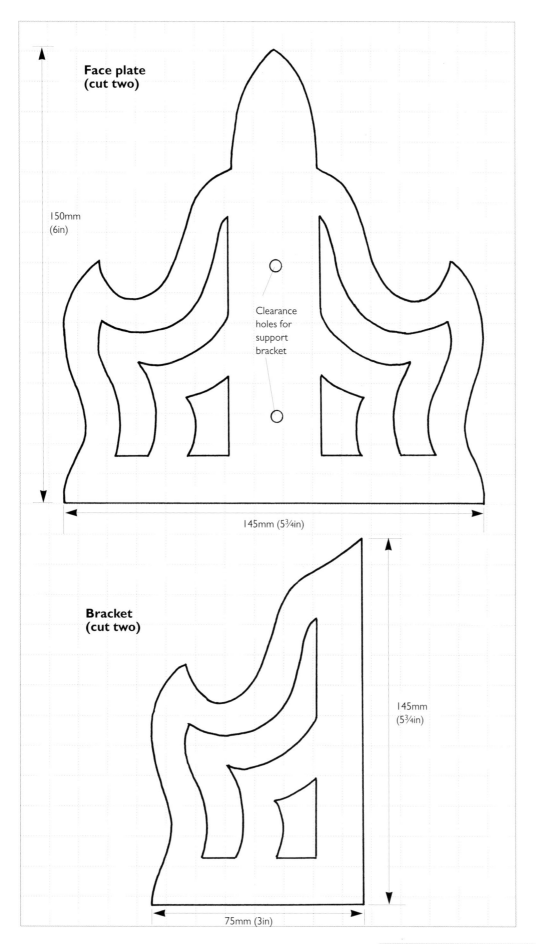

**Face plate
(cut two)**

150mm
(6in)

Clearance
holes for
support
bracket

145mm (5¾in)

**Bracket
(cut two)**

145mm
(5¾in)

75mm (3in)

This template needs to be enlarged by 125%
1 square = 1 cm

Hanging basket bracket

This item is straightforward to make. The project consists of two parts – the bracket itself and the back panel to which it is fixed. This design uses an ivy leaf motif and, when painted and varnished, adds a little colour of its own to the completed ensemble.

The example was made from some offcuts of 20mm (¾in) flooring grade plywood. Plywood is essential for this project, as the material used needs to have enough strength to support a hanging basket in all weathers and especially when wet. A large basket full of plants, soil and water can easily weigh 10 kilograms or so. The templates allow for a fairly large basket, around 450mm (17¾in) in diameter. You can make the bracket larger or smaller if you wish. The instructions show how to make a pair of brackets, but you could just as easily make one. The stack created by two pieces of 20mm (¾in) plywood may be beyond the capacity of many saws, if this is the case saw one at a time. You will find that the blade will cut quite quickly through the 20mm (¾in) thickness of the plywood so be careful not to let it run away with itself.

EQUIPMENT AND MATERIALS

- 2 pieces of 20mm (¾in) plywood, 270mm x 120mm (10⅝in x 4¾in), for the back supports
- 2 pieces, 205mm x 190mm (8¹⁄₁₆in x 7½in) from the same material, for the brackets
- 4 woodscrews, preferably brass ones, No. 8 50mm (2in)

- 6 woodscrews No. 8 38mm (1½in) for fixing the bracket to its back support
- Drill bits, to drill pilot and clearance holes for woodscrews, see chart on page 8
- Wood glue, for fixing the bracket to its support
- Paint and varnish, to decorate and protect from the elements

A fairly coarse saw blade such as a No. 12 skip-tooth blade or similar. You could also use a coping saw blade for this project.

TEMPLATES

Back support	78
Bracket	78

1 Make a copy of the cutting patterns for the bracket and the back support. Make two sets of blanks. If your scrollsaw can cope with a double thickness of plywood, attach each pair of blanks together with double-sided adhesive tape. Fix the cutting patterns on top of each set of blanks with spray mount.

2 Drill the starter holes in the bracket to make the two internal cutouts. Use a 3mm (⁷⁄₆₄in) drill because the larger scrollsaw blade will need a little more space to pass through the blank.

3 Set up the scrollsaw and thread the blade through the first of the starter holes and fix the hold down device. With plywood as thick as 20mm (¾in), a hold down may be helpful, especially when turning sharp corners. You can cut away

◄ Using pieces of double-sided adhesive tape to make a stack so two brackets can be cut out at the same time.

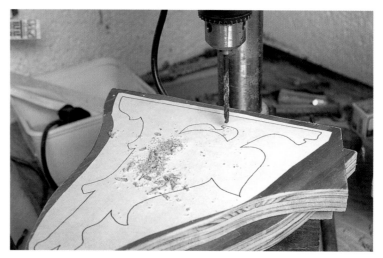

▲ Drilling starter holes for the internal cutouts.

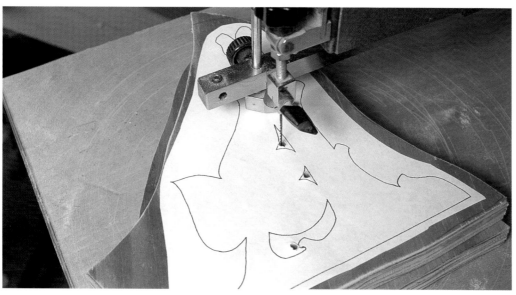

◄ The scrollsaw set up ready to make the internal cutouts on the bracket.

▲ Close-up of the missing ply section.

► Filing the filler to shape, to make up for the missing plywood.

the waste from the pattern in sections, to allow you to come up to the cutting line again, particularly at the sharp corners. Which ever way you choose to work, make the internal cuts and reset the saw to make the external cuts on both pieces.

4 Cut around the outside of the patterns of both pieces and repeat if you intend making a pair of the brackets.

5 It is common to find gaps in plywood. These can be filled with either wood filler or plastic padding (as was used here), and then filed and sanded into shape once the filler has set hard. Make any small repairs that are necessary.

6 Drill five clearance holes in each of the back supports (see template for positions). Three of the holes are for the

► Countersinking the fixing holes on the back support after drilling.

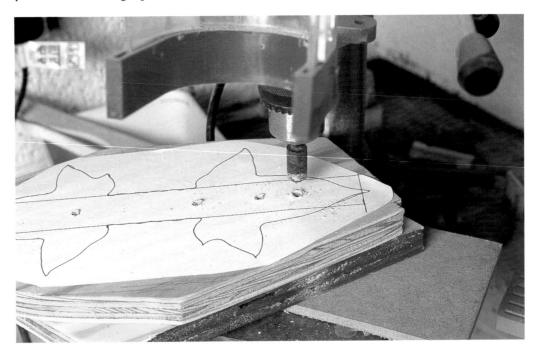

woodscrews which fix the bracket to the support plate and the remaining two are used to fix the completed assembly to the wall. Countersink the two wall fixing holes from the front of the back support and the three fixing holes for attaching the support plate to the bracket from the reverse side of the back support.

7 Place the bracket on the back support and mark the position of the fixing holes on the bracket. Drill pilot holes for the No. 8 woodscrews. Apply a smear of wood glue to the back edge of the bracket and join the two pieces together with the woodscrews. Leave for a short time so the glue sets properly.

8 Support the completed assembly so you can round down the edges of the plywood where the hanging basket will hang. This will avoid undue wear and tear to either the bracket or the hanging basket wire. Simply sand or file away the edges of the plywood to round it off enough to leave no sharp edges.

9 Decorate the completed project. I would recommend an undercoat of acrylic primer. Once this has dried thoroughly, sand off any roughness and proceed with the decoration. The example was painted with Humbrol enamels. Deep green was used for the ivy leaves and mid-brown for the rest. Finish

off the job with three good coats of exterior varnish and allow to dry thoroughly before fitting.

▲ Filing the edges where the hanging basket wire will fit on the bracket.

▲ The assembled pair of brackets ready for final decoration.

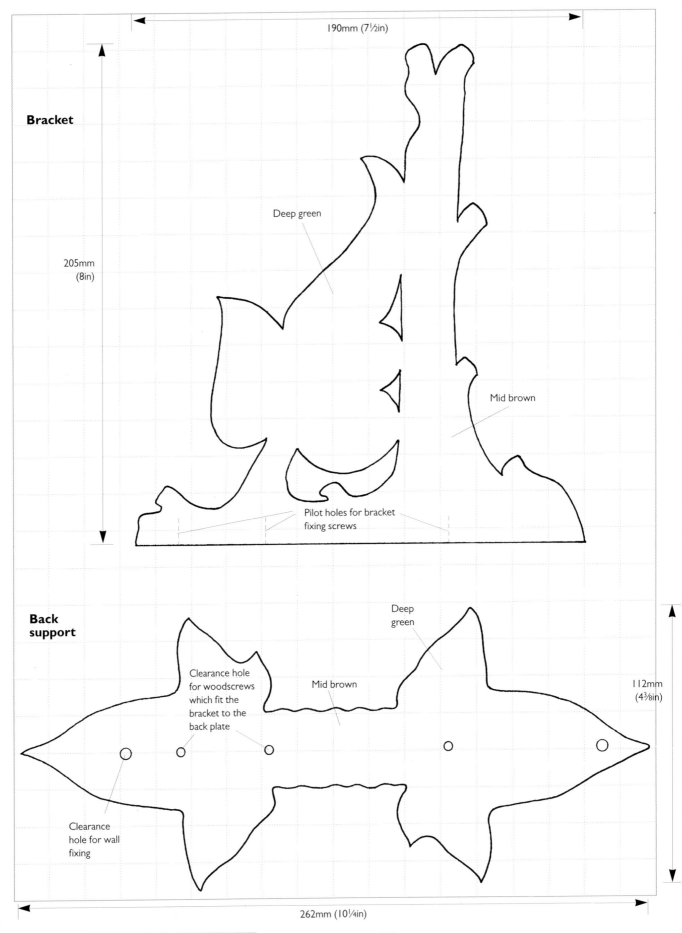

Bracket

190mm (7½in)

205mm
(8in)

Deep green

Mid brown

Pilot holes for bracket
fixing screws

**Back
support**

Deep
green

Clearance hole
for woodscrews
which fit the
bracket to the
back plate

Mid brown

112mm
(4⅜in)

Clearance
hole for wall
fixing

262mm (10¼in)

This template needs to be enlarged by 153%
1 square = 1.5 cm

Magazine rack

This free-standing magazine rack was built in order to free the coffee table from the clutter of papers and magazines. The rack consists of two support struts, a base and two matching scroll-cut side panels, both decorated with a seaside scene. The support struts are cut on the scroll-saw to resemble breaking waves. The rack is slightly bigger than A4, with the ends left open ended to accommodate different magazine and newspaper sizes.

The project will allow you to practise cutting intricate shapes as well as straight lines on the scrollsaw, using different blades for the different types of material. The support struts are made from pine and are cut using a No. 5 blade. The side panels and base are cut from MDF with a No. 7 skip-tooth blade. Don't forget to wear your dust mask, particularly when cutting the MDF material.

EQUIPMENT AND MATERIALS

- 2 pieces of pine board, 230mm x 310mm (9in x 12¼in) and 20mm (¾in) thick
- 1 piece of 6mm (¼in) MDF or plywood, 320mm x 91mm (12⅝in x 3¹⁰⁄₁₆in), for the base
- 2 pieces of 6mm (¼in) MDF, 217mm x 332mm (8⁹⁄₁₆in x 13⅛in), for the side panels
- Panel pins
- Nail punch and light hammer
- Wood glue
- Paint and polish

SCROLLSAW BLADE
No. 7 skip-tooth blade
No. 5 general purpose blade

TEMPLATES	
Support strut	83
Base	84
Side panel	85

1 Make up the three cutting patterns. Cut blanks for the side panels from MDF. Sand off any rough edges.

▲ Using double-sided adhesive tape to attach two blanks together for stack sawing.

► Drilling the starter holes ready to make the internal cutouts.

2 Using some small pieces of double-sided adhesive tape, fix the two panel blanks together to form a stack. Try to remember to stick the double-sided adhesive tape in the waste areas of the blanks, so that you will not have any problems separating the two panels once all the cutting out has been completed.

3 Mark and drill starter holes for the internal cutouts on the panel. Drill, where possible, at a corner or sharp angle so that the start and finish of the cut will meet up easily. Drill the nail starter holes in the ends of each panel (as marked on the template).

4 Set up the scrollsaw with the No. 7 skip-tooth blade and check the hold down device is correctly set for the 12mm

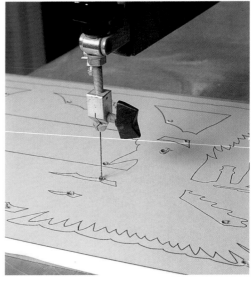

▲ The scrollsaw blade threaded and ready to make the internal cuts.

◀ Close up of side panel from the bottom of the stack, showing typical saw tearout after cutting. This is removed carefully with fine sandpaper.

(½in) sandwich of MDF. Make the internal cuts. Reset the scrollsaw, making sure the tension is correct, to make the external cut which will free the two panels from the waste material. Carefully clean any saw tearout off the panels with a piece of fine sandpaper, taking particular care when sanding delicate areas, such as the feathers of the seagull.

5 The two support struts are made from 20mm (¾in) thick pine board. Other woods and thicknesses may be used, but take care not to use too thin a piece of wood or the support strength may be impaired. Align the grain of the wood so that it runs vertically. This will give maximum strength in the direction likely to receive most stress. Cut the support struts with a standard No. 5 blade. The struts can also be stack sawn, providing your saw can cut a 40mm (1⅝in) thickness. If not, copy the cutting pattern so you have two copies, and cut the end struts individually. After cutting, clean up the two pieces. Do not discard the waste pieces of wood from inside the wave pattern on the outside of each support strut, as these will be needed again at a later stage.

▼ Showing the starter cut for the support struts. Starting on a straight line will make it easier to meet up the start and finish of the cut.

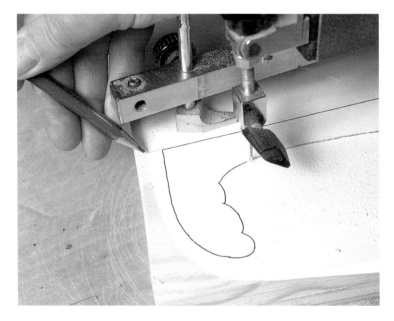

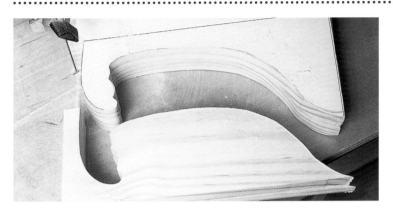

▲ Fitting the waste material back together with the support strut to create a level surface for the side panel.

6 Decorate the side panels. The panels shown were painted with white acrylic primer and allowed to dry. The panels were given a light rub down on both sides with sandpaper. Humbrol light blue enamel was applied. When this was dry, the panels were turned over, so that the other side could be painted. You will find that the paint will soak into the cut edges considerably more than on the face of the sheet, so it's worth painting the sides twice, ensuring an even coating of paint all over the panels.

7 Take the support struts, together with the waste pieces cut from the wave pattern on the outside of each strut. The waste pieces can act as a support for the struts while you punch the nails home. Fit the waste material back together with the support strut and lay one of the side panels into position ready for nailing. Put the second support strut under the other end of the side panel, so that the panel is level. Apply a smear of glue to the inner surface of the support strut. Tap the nails home using the nail punch to avoid scarring the painted surface of the side panel. Turn the panel around and attach the second support strut. Attach the second side panel by repeating the whole procedure.

8 Cut the base panel using the dimensions given in the template. Drill pilot holes in the positions indicated. Apply a little glue beneath the ends of the base panel. Punch home the panel pins with a nail punch. Once the glue has dried thoroughly, polish the support struts with wax polish or any other finish of your choice.

► Punching in the panel pins to secure the side panels to the support struts.

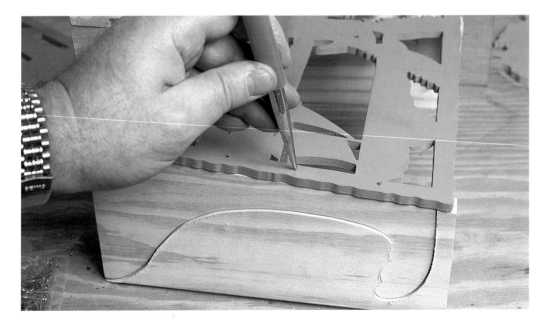

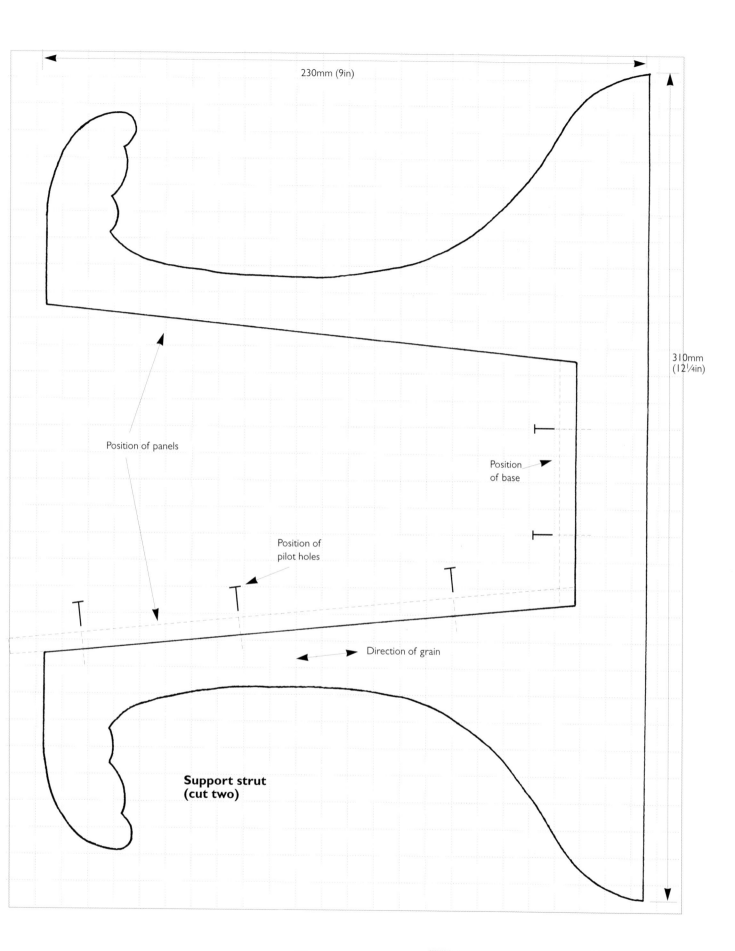

230mm (9in)

310mm
(12¼in)

Position of panels

Position of base

Position of
pilot holes

Direction of grain

**Support strut
(cut two)**

This template needs to be enlarged by 140%
1 square = 1cm

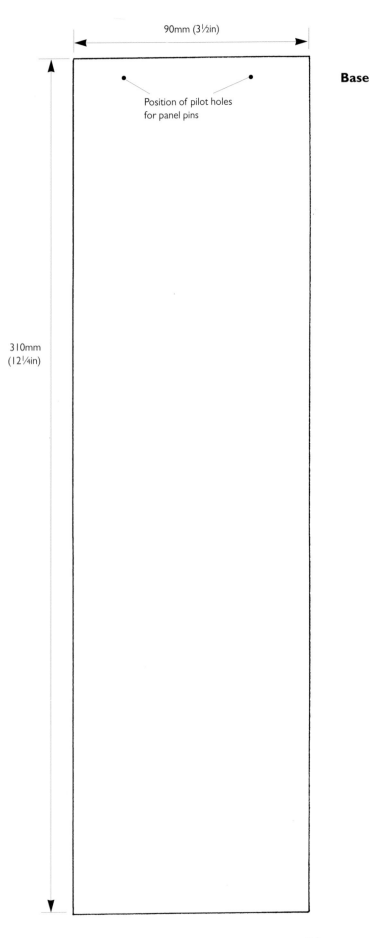

90mm (3½in)

Base

Position of pilot holes
for panel pins

310mm
(12¼in)

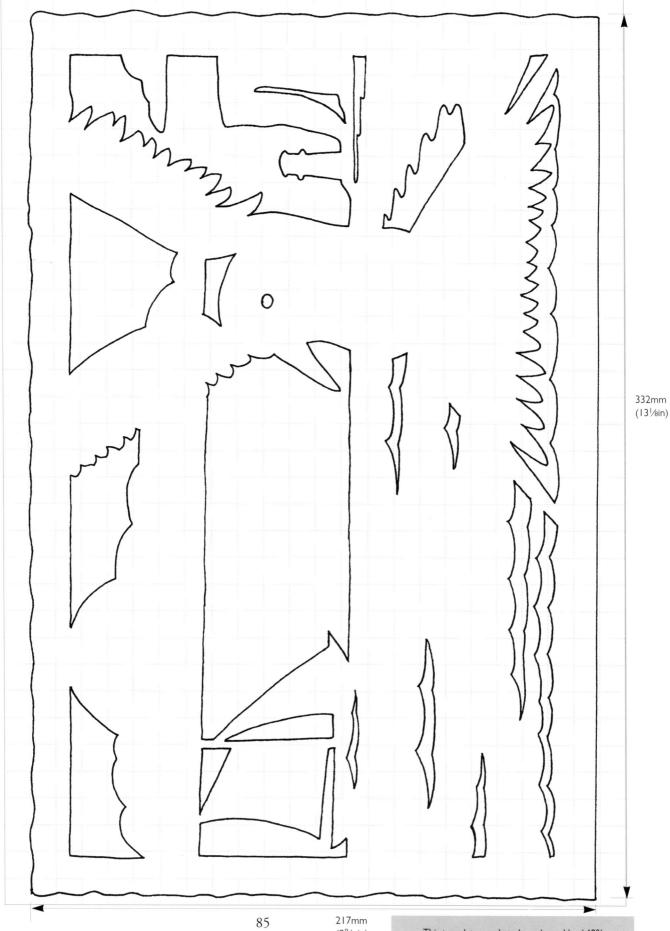

332mm
(13⅛in)

85

Side panel (cut two)

217mm
(8⁹⁄₁₆in)

This template needs to be enlarged by 140%
1 square = 1cm

Curtain tie brackets

This project can be made from offcuts of valuable wood left over from other projects. I used two small offcuts of mahogany and some good oak reclaimed from an old chest that was beyond economic repair. The layered curtain tie uses the contrasting colours of two different woods. No decoration is needed once the parts have been assembled, other than an application of polish to give the finished plates a lovely warm glow. The materials and instructions given will make a matching pair of curtain tie brackets.

Although the instructions suggest stack sawing the pieces, I cut the pieces individually. I did not have enough wood to make blanks of roughly the same size, instead I had to fit the pattern carefully, making stack sawing impossible.

EQUIPMENT AND MATERIALS

- 2 pieces of wood, about 180mm x 210mm (7in x 8¼in)
- 2 pieces of wood in a contrasting colour, about 80mm x 80mm (3⅛in x 3⅛in)

(By moving the cutting patterns around you may find you need less wood than this, the points of the design can be interlocked so that almost nothing is wasted.)

- Drill bit, to drill clearance holes for hooks, see chart on page 8
- 2 brass hooks
- Wood glue
- Furniture polish, such as wax polish or french polish

1 Make up copies of the two cutting patterns. Only two will be required as both backing plates and bosses can be stack sawn. The resulting stack will only be around 12mm (½in), well within the capabilities of even a modest scrollsaw. Carry out any surface preparation before you start. The design is rather spiky, making sanding after the pieces have been cut rather difficult. Cut out two blank pieces of wood and attach them together using double-sided adhesive tape. Remember to try and place the adhesive tape in waste areas of the blank. Stick the cutting pattern in place on the top blank with spray mount.

2 Drill the clearance hole in the two back plates, as shown on the template, for the curtain hooks.

3 Set up the saw with the No. 7 plain blade and set the hold down device. It will be easier to cut in from the outside of the blank, rather than try to follow the outline of the pattern in one continuous cut. Cut into a point, back the blade out and make another cut into the point,

▲ Carrying out surface preparation on the oak blanks prior to cutting, to avoid problems after cutting has been completed.

◀ Drilling the hook clearance holes in the back plates.

► Cutting out the back plate by removing small sections of waste material, so maintaining the sharpness of the design.

▼ The completed curtain tie brackets resting on scraps of wood while the glue sets. The curtain hooks are being used to maintain hole alignment while the glue dries. The scraps of wood lift the curtain ties above the level of the bench ensuring the bottom of the hook screw is clear of the bench.

cutting pattern to the top of the stack with spray mount. Drill the clearance hole for the curtain hooks in the centre (see template for position). Set up the saw to cut the two bosses. Check the hold down device. Make the cut around the line of the cutting pattern, remembering that the blade will cut faster across the grain than along it. This point is particularly important, as the piece is small and any cutting errors will be much more obvious than they would be in larger pieces. Clean up the bosses by sanding lightly.

5 The bosses now need to be glued to their back plates to make up the completed curtain tie bracket. Carefully align the two parts of each bracket (as shown on the template), ensuring that the centre holes line up. Apply a smear of wood glue to the back of the boss, taking care not to get glue too close to the central hole, as glue here will prevent the hook from being screwed through the hole easily. Fit a short length of knitting needle or nail of appropriate diameter, or use the curtain hooks as I have done, into the holes while the glue sets. This will ensure that the holes stay aligned. Repeat the procedure for the bracket and allow the glue to set completely.

slicing out part of the waste material. In this way, you will be able to maintain the sharpness of each point without having to worry about turning the blade back on itself to make the adjacent cut. Carry on round the design until you have completed all the cuts. A little light sanding on the back of the plates may be needed to remove any saw tearout.

4 Cut two blanks for the bosses and attach them to each other with double-sided adhesive tape, and stick the

6 Polish or finish the completed curtain tie brackets in whatever way you feel appropriate. That done, they are ready to be fitted in place.

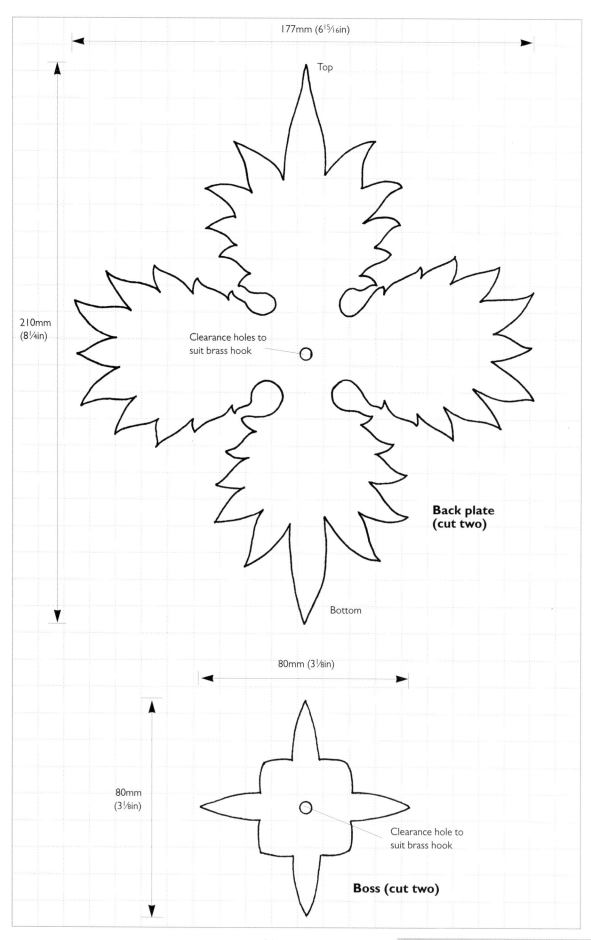

177mm (6¹⁵⁄₁₆in)

Top

210mm
(8¼in)

Clearance holes to
suit brass hook

**Back plate
(cut two)**

Bottom

80mm (3⅛in)

80mm
(3⅛in)

Clearance hole to
suit brass hook

Boss (cut two)

This template needs to be enlarged by 140%
1 square = 1cm

Position of boss on back plate

Picture frame

The internal cutout on this frame is bevel cut on the scrollsaw, providing a useful exercise in cutting at an angle. Don't despair if your saw does not have a tilting table as it is very simple to make up a frame for the workpiece to sit on at the correct angle. A few pieces of scrap timber are all you will need to make up a jig to do the job (see page 18 for details).

The picture frame is made out of two pieces – the frame and the retaining frame which goes behind it, to hold the glass and picture in place. The design has a square aperture for the picture, but the outer curves can be elongated to make the design suitable for a portrait shape or a landscape-shaped picture. The overall size can be scaled up and down to fit any size of picture you want. The examples shown have an outside measurement of 200mm (7⅞in) square for a picture size of 120mm (4¾in) square.

EQUIPMENT AND MATERIALS

- 6mm (¼in) thick MDF, 200mm (7⅞in) square
- 3mm (⅛in) thick plywood or MDF, 165mm (6½in) square
- Glass or transparent acrylic sheets, 125mm (5in) square
- Backing card, 125mm (5in) square
- Picture frame screw eyes
- Length of picture wire or string
- Masking tape
- Wood glue
- Decorating materials

(If you do not have a tilting table you will need a piece of scrap timber for a jig.)

SCROLLSAW BLADE	TEMPLATES	
No. 7 skip-tooth blade	Frame	95
	Retaining frame	96

▲ Using the cutting pattern as a template to mark out MDF blanks.

▼ *Below* The scrollsaw set up ready to begin the bevel cut.

▶ *Below right* The bevel cut nearing completion.

1 Make up the cutting patterns to whatever dimensions you have chosen for your picture frame. Cut a blank and attach the pattern to it. The side of the blank facing upwards, with the pattern attached, will become the back of the frame. If you are using plywood, one side of the wood may have a better surface or colour than the other, so choose which side of the wood you wish to be displayed at this point. Drill a starter hole for the saw blade. The saw

blade will have to enter the starter hole at an angle, so the hole will need to be quite a bit larger than normal. If the hole is too small the blade will get distorted.

2 If you do not have a tilting table, make the jig using the template. If your saw has a tilting work table, then set it carefully to 30 degrees. Check the angle by setting a protractor against the saw table.

3 Thread the blade through the starter hole. It is likely that the hold down device will be either difficult or impossible to set for a bevel cut, so you will have to be more careful when cutting the workpiece, particularly when guiding the blade around corners. Once you have completed the internal cutout, remove the workpiece from the saw and return the table to the horizontal position, ready for the outside cut. If there are any small inaccuracies in the bevel cut, smooth them out with sandpaper.

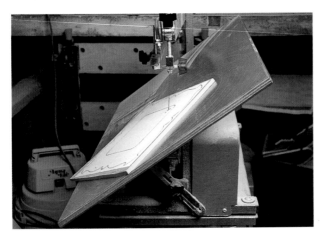

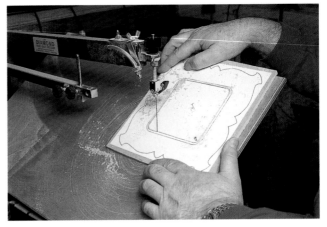

▲ The scrollsaw set up and making the outside cut of the main frame.

▲ The scrollsaw set up ready to make the internal cut in the retaining frames.

4 Make the external cut following the pattern. Begin and end at a corner so that the cut meets up easily. Once you have completed the cut sand away any saw tearout carefully.

5 Cut a blank for the retaining frame and attach the cutting pattern to it using spray mount. Drill a starter hole for the internal cutout and set up your saw. This time you will be able to use the hold down device as normal. Make the internal cutout and complete the retaining frame with the external cut. Make sure that the retaining frame is not visible from the front of the completed frame. If it is, then reduce the width of the retaining frame.

6 Glue the retaining frame in place behind the picture frame. Make certain the bevel cut on the frame is the right way round. Clamp the pieces in place while the glue dries. If you don't

◀ Gluing the picture retaining frames in position on the back of each frame.

▲ Two decorated frames ready for final assembly.

► Cutting picture wire to length. Pass the wire through the screw eye and twist round on itself so no rough ends are left.

easily. Check the piece for size in the frame and file or sand it down if it is too big. Check the size of the picture you want to mount, then cut some backing card to the same size as the glass.

8 Decorate your frame with a finish of your choice. One of the examples shown was given a coat of primer, then sprayed with metallic gold paint. The other frame was finished with a craft kit to give an antique wood effect.

9 When the paint or finish you have used is dry, fit the glass, picture and backing card. The glass or transparent acrylic sheet goes in first and can be secured with a little glue in the corners. This will avoid any strain being placed on the masking tape used to hold the picture and backing card. Before you actually insert the picture, make very sure there are no marks, smudges or pieces of dust on the inside of the glass, or you will have to remove the picture and start again. When you are satisfied that the glass is clean, position your picture, fit the backing card and secure with masking tape all round.

happen to have any suitable clamps, use some scrap wood or reasonably heavy item.

7 Once the adhesive has set thoroughly, measure and mark 125mm (5in) square on the glass or transparent acrylic sheet. If you are using transparent acrylic as was the case in the example, leave the protective film in place and use a craft knife to score the sheet on both sides. The square required can then be snapped off

10 Measure an equal distance down each side of the retaining frame and make a pilot hole for the screw eyes. Screw the eyes into position, making sure they are the right way round for the picture. Cut off a length of picture wire or string and fix it to the screw eyes.

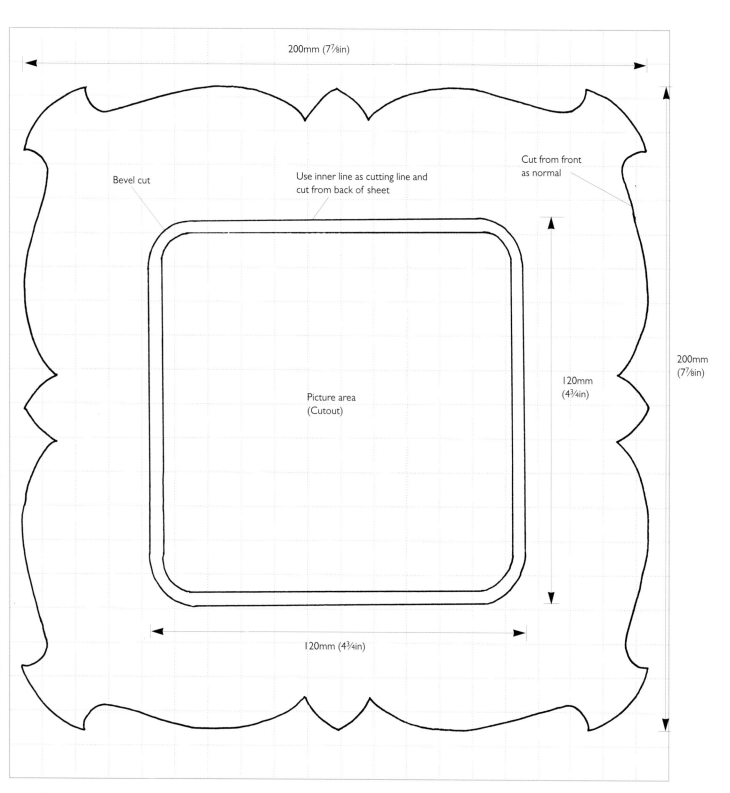

200mm (7⅞in)

Cut from front
as normal

Bevel cut

Use inner line as cutting line and
cut from back of sheet

200mm
(7⅞in)

120mm
(4¾in)

Picture area
(Cutout)

120mm (4¾in)

Frame

This template needs to be enlarged by 165%
1 square = 1.5cm

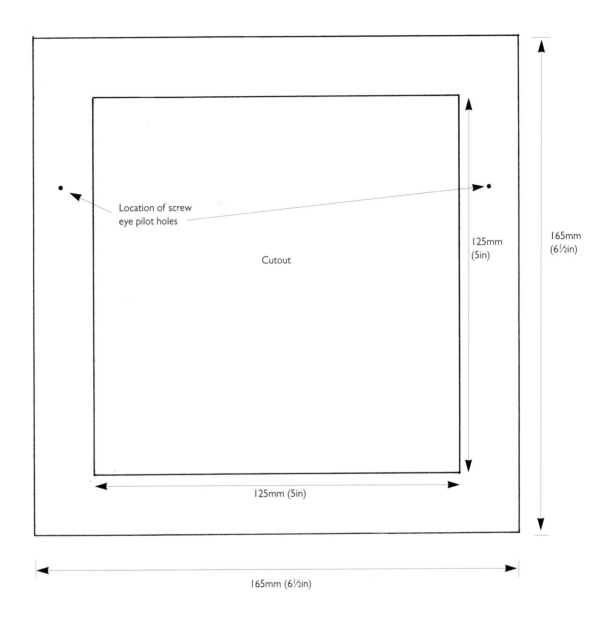

Location of screw
eye pilot holes

Cutout

125mm
(5in)

165mm
(6½in)

125mm (5in)

165mm (6½in)

Retaining frame

Victorian gingerbread

The Victorian era saw an increase in ornate decoration and embellishment. This project comprises a suite of decorative additions which will add a little extra interest to otherwise plain items such as doors, cupboards, wooden chests, boxes. The design makes a set of four corners and one centrepiece which can be glued or pinned onto whatever takes your fancy. The finishes used can be anything from Humbrol metallic gunmetal paint, with brass pins to simulate wrought iron, to bright colours, to add a cheery touch to drab cupboards.

The individual parts of this project are quite small (you can make them any size you want of course), so you will be able to use up the bits and pieces left over from other projects. Cutting is simple as there are no internal cutouts. You can use almost any sort of sheet material you happen to have to make up these items. You could even set up your scrollsaw with a metal cutting blade and make them from sheet brass.

EQUIPMENT AND MATERIALS

- 4 pieces of 6mm (¼in) MDF or similar, 108mm (4¼in) square
- 1 piece of 6mm (¼in) MDF or similar, 216mm x 60mm (8½in x 2⅜in)

(These are the maximum dimensions of the finished pieces. You can arrange the layout of the corner pieces on your sheet of material so you make best possible use of a relatively small piece of sheet material.)

- Decorating materials of your choice
- Brass panel pins, if you would like to mount the pieces this way
- Drill bits, to drill clearance holes for panel pins, see chart on page 8

SCROLLSAW BLADE		TEMPLATES	
No. 7 skip-tooth saw blade		Centrepiece	100
		Corner pieces	100

▶ Using the cutting patterns as templates to mark out the blanks for the corner and centre piece on a spare piece of 6mm (¼in) MDF.

1 Make up a set of cutting patterns, scaling the pieces up or down as you wish. It is easier to make up two corner patterns to every one pattern for the centrepiece.

▼ The scrollsaw set up to cut out a stack of corners.

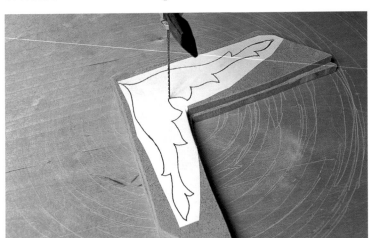

2 Make up as many blanks as you need. The pieces can be stack sawn together. If you are using 6mm (¼in) material such as MDF, the practical limit is probably three blanks stacked together. More than three in a stack and you may find that the pieces slip around during cutting. Use a new blade to cut a stack of three. You can, of course, use nails to hold the stack together if you have sufficient waste material, otherwise use double-sided adhesive tape.

3 Fix the cutting patterns in place on top of the stack with spray mount. Set up your scrollsaw and cut around the outlines carefully. It will be difficult to use a hold down device with such small

blanks. When using small offcuts, with not much spare material surrounding the cutting line, you must take extra care not to get your fingers in the way of the blade. Once you have finished cutting all the pieces you require, sand off any saw tearout with fine sandpaper.

4 Decorate the finished parts. For the example shown, I used the Humbrol enamel range of paints. A coat of white acrylic primer was applied and then lightly sanded before applying the colour coat. One set of corners and a centre piece were drilled with pilot holes for the brass pins before being painted with gunmetal finish. The brass pins contrast well with the dark grey paint which gives the appearance of wrought iron when dry completely.

5 Installing these gingerbread pieces can be accomplished quite easily by gluing them into position. You can also use the brass pins for effect. For maximum strength you can always glue and pin areas which might be subject to wear and tear.

▲ A selection of gingerbread pieces ready for painting.

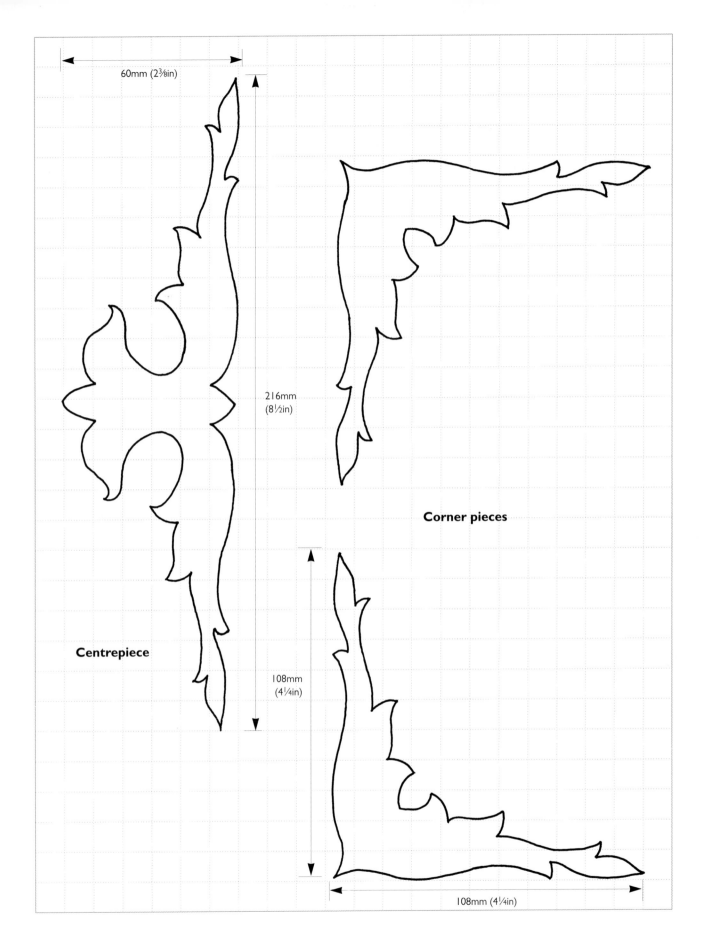

60mm (2⅜in)

216mm
(8½in)

108mm
(4¼in)

108mm (4¼in)

Corner pieces

Centrepiece

This template needs to be enlarged by 125%
1 square = 1cm

Book rest

This project, while supporting most sizes of book quite adequately, is a genuine flat-pack item. It comes apart and can be reassembled in seconds, needing no nails, screws, glue or anything else to keep it together. The book rest consists of five pieces – a book panel, two feet, that also act as a support for the base of the book, and a couple of brackets which support the book panel and lock everything together.

The example was made from 6mm (¼in) MDF for the book panel, 9mm (⅜in) MDF for the locking brackets, and 18mm x 72mm (¾in x 2¾in) pine for the feet. You can of course use other materials if you prefer, but if you are using different thicknesses of material, remember to adjust the slots in the feet accordingly.

EQUIPMENT AND MATERIALS

- 6mm (¼in) MDF, 225mm x 280mm (8⅞in x 9in), for the main panel
- 2 pieces of 9mm (⅜in) MDF, 170mm x 168mm (6¾in x 6⅝in), for the locking brackets
These brackets being roughly triangular in shape can be cut from a single piece of MDF, not much larger than the sizes given for each individual bracket.

- 2 pieces of 18mm (¾in) pine, 72mm x 230mm (2¹³⁄₁₆in x 9in), for the locking brackets
- Drill bit to make starter hole (the size of bit is not critical as there are no small internal cutouts)
- Decorating materials of your choice

SCROLLSAW BLADE
No. 7 skip-tooth blade, for the MDF
No. 10 general purpose blade, for the pine

TEMPLATES	
Book panel	105
Bracket	106
Feet	106

► Marking the starter hole positions on the book panel before drilling.

▼ The scrollsaw set up to make the internal cutouts in the book panel.

1 Make up the three cutting patterns to the sizes shown or modify them if you wish. If you intend changing the dimensions, or are using different thicknesses of material, remember to change the size of the slots in the book panel. Mark and cut blanks from 6mm (¼in) and 9mm (⅜in) MDF. Cut out the pine blanks.

2 The blanks for the brackets and feet can be made up into stacks, so that two pieces can be cut at the same time. Use double-sided adhesive tape to attach the blanks together, making sure you put the tape in the waste areas. The brackets will make a stack of 18mm (¾in) in height which is well within the capacity of almost any scrollsaw, and the pine makes a stack of 36mm (1½in).

3 Mark and drill clearance holes in the book panel. Fit the skip-tooth blade and set the hold down device. Make the outside cut first, this will make the book panel easier to handle on a smaller

◄ Cutting out the two brackets together by stack sawing. This ensures they will both be precisely the same shape when cutting is completed.

scrollsaw. Then make the internal cutouts. Take good care to follow the lines on the cutting pattern precisely, making the curves smooth and the lines straight. As the column pattern is repeated, any discrepancies will show up. Once you have completed the cutting of the main panel, sand off any saw tearout from the back of the panel.

4 Cut out the brackets. Do this while the skip-tooth blade is fitted. The brackets are a straight-forward external cut, but make sure you cut accurately as a close fit is needed to make all the parts of the completed project lock together. When you have cut out the two brackets, clean up any saw tearout.

5 Cut the feet from the pine, making sure the grain runs along the length of the two pieces. Drill a starter hole for the joint, which is a mortice-type slot. Set

up your saw with the No. 10 general purpose blade. Remember, when cutting softwoods, such as pine, that the blade will cut much faster across the grain than along it. Cut out the sockets first and then refit your blade to make the simple external cut. The feet need to be tapered

▼ A coarse blade set up in the scrollsaw ready for cutting out the pine feet for the book. This type of blade will enable faster cutting to be carried out along the grain of the pine.

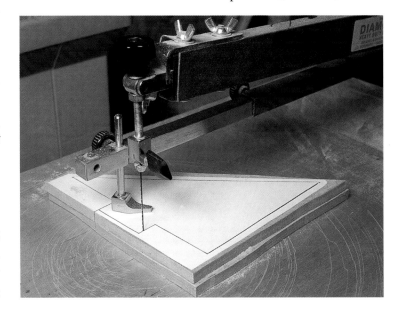

► Checking to see if all the parts of the book rest fit together properly.

to allow the panel to lean backwards sufficiently to prevent the book from slipping off the stand. This can be done on the scrollsaw, or using a plane or a belt sander. Use whatever you have available and then sand the feet smooth ready for decoration.

6 Put the five parts of the book rest together to test for fit before you decorate. Make sure the pieces fit firmly. Make any small adjustments that may be needed, such as trimming the angle at the back of the feet. Don't forget to allow for a thickness of paint, if you intend painting the final piece. Decorate the book rest. When all the paint, varnish or whatever you have used has dried thoroughly, check again that everything will fit together properly.

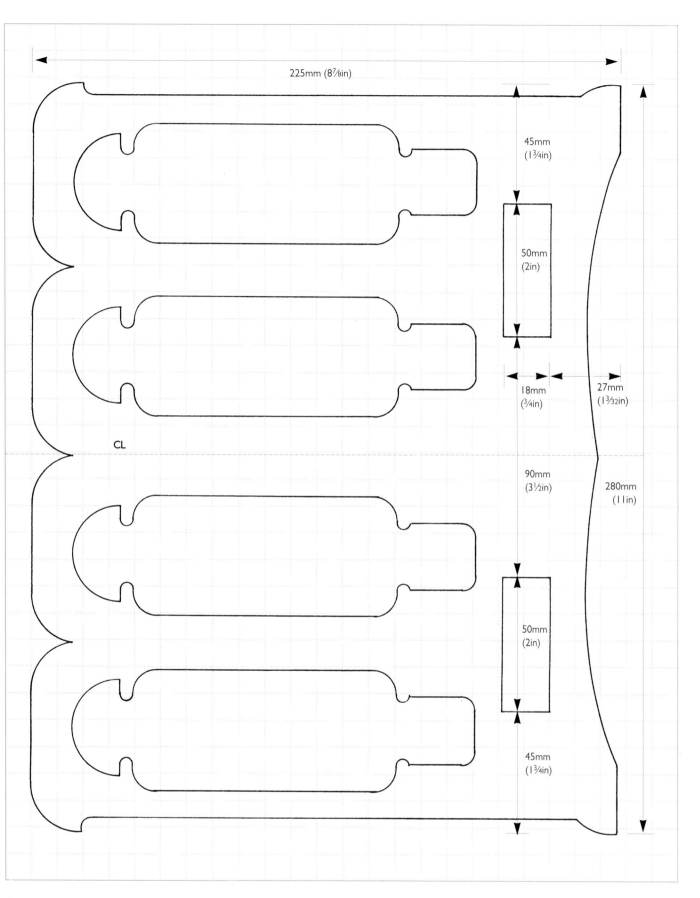

225mm (8⅞in)

45mm
(1¾in)

50mm
(2in)

18mm
(¾in)

27mm
(1³⁄₃₂in)

CL

90mm
(3½in)

280mm
(11in)

50mm
(2in)

45mm
(1¾in)

Book panel

This template needs to be enlarged by 140%
1 square = 1cm

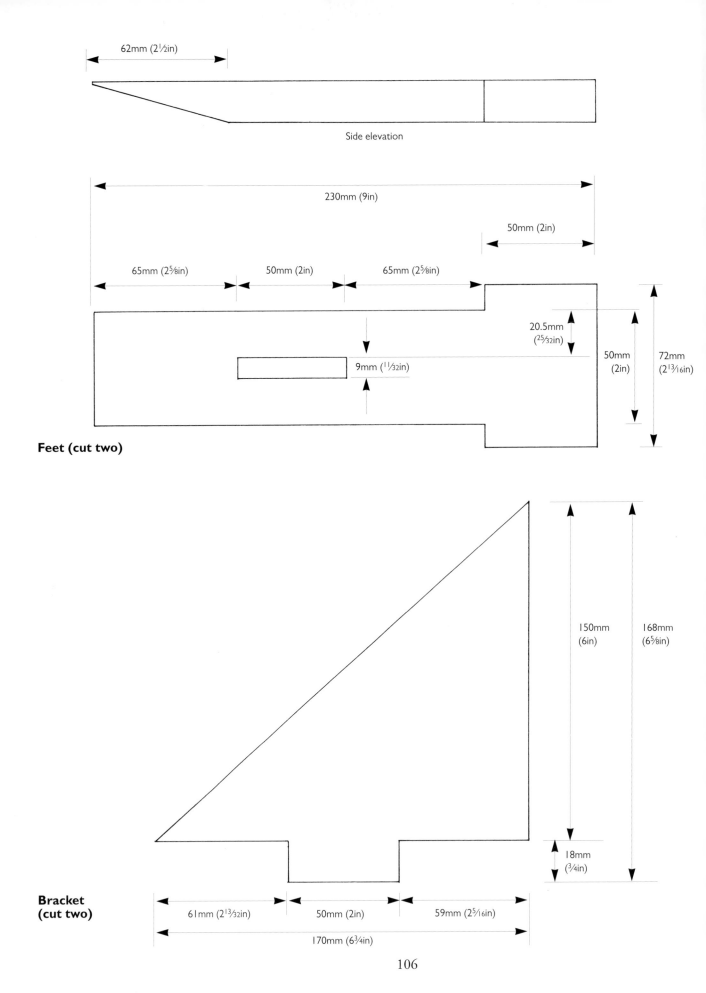

62mm (2½in)

Side elevation

230mm (9in)

50mm (2in)

65mm (2⅝in)

50mm (2in)

65mm (2⅝in)

20.5mm (²⁵⁄₃₂in)

9mm (¹¹⁄₃₂in)

50mm (2in)

72mm (2¹³⁄₁₆in)

Feet (cut two)

150mm (6in)

168mm (6⅝in)

18mm (¾in)

Bracket (cut two)

61mm (2¹³⁄₃₂in)

50mm (2in)

59mm (2⁵⁄₁₆in)

170mm (6¾in)

Vine leaf clock

This project consists of one scroll-cut panel, but is fairly intricate and will require patience, careful cutting and a slender blade. Good control of the workpiece is also called for as it is easy to allow the saw to overrun, especially on the smaller internal cutouts of the design. The project is completed with detailed decoration, then the clock face and quartz movement are fitted. In this instance, if you intend to use the items specified, such as the 100mm (4in) brass clock face, it is important to stick closely to the dimensions given when making up the cutting pattern, so that everything will fit correctly.

EQUIPMENT AND MATERIALS

- Sheet material such as MDF, 6mm (¼in) thick, 190mm (7½in) square
- An appropriate drill for the spindle hole
- 2mm (³⁄₃₂in) drill bit to make the starter holes for the internal cutouts.
- Clock movement, hand set and 100mm (4in) clock face
- Carbon paper
- Paints and varnish, for decoration
- Two-part epoxy adhesive, to fix the dial in place

SCROLLSAW BLADE

No. 5 skip-tooth blade

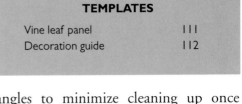

TEMPLATES

Vine leaf panel	111
Decoration guide	112

1 Make up a cutting pattern from the template. Attach the pattern to a 6mm (¼in) sheet material with spray mount.

2 Carefully drill the starter holes for the internal cutouts using a 2mm (³⁄₃₂in) drill bit and drill close to sharp

▲ Drilling the spindle hole in the panel. It is important to ensure this hole is truly vertical, hence the use of a bench drill.

▶ The scrollsaw set up to make the intricate internal cutouts.

angles to minimize cleaning up once cutting has been completed.

3 Fit an appropriate drill bit (I used 8mm (⁵⁄₁₆in)) into your drill and make the spindle hole. If you are using a different type of clock movement, check the diameter of the spindle.

4 Thread the fine skip-tooth blade through a starter hole. Check that the blade tension is set correctly and that the hold down is set as close to the workpiece as possible without snagging on the blade. With the smaller internal cuts, it is advisable to make one side of the cut into a sharp corner and then back the blade out to the starter hole and come in again from the other side to complete

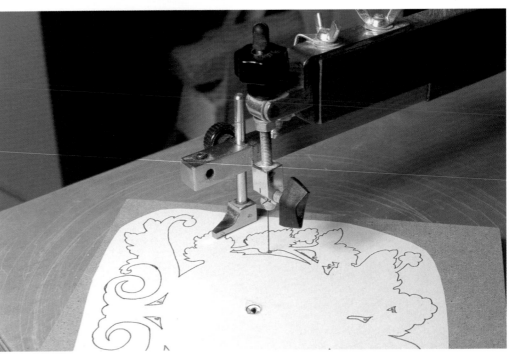

the cut. This procedure will allow you to maintain the sharpness of the corners and avoid turning the blade round on itself in a confined space.

5 Set up your saw to make the external cut around the panel. Again, some degree of care will be needed to avoid undue strain on vulnerable areas of the design, such as the bunches of grapes at the top of the clock, and the scrolls at the bottom of the panel. Make sure the blade tension is correct and the hold down is set properly. Make sure you have full control over the workpiece, so that the saw does not overrun and cut into the design.

6 Having successfully completed the external cut, very lightly and carefully sand off any saw tearout from the back of the clock panel. A set of needle files can be used to clean up the small niches, particularly around some of the internal cutouts. A half-round file or small craft knife, used carefully, will clear up any rough edges.

7 Give the panel a coat of white acrylic primer. A fairly small brush will be needed for this operation. A nylon brush works best, as it has slightly stiffer bristles which allows it to push the acrylic primer into small crevices.

8 Once the primer has dried (which usually takes about an hour) lightly rub the panel down with fine sandpaper. The panel is now ready for decorating. To make things simple, make up a full-size

▲ The internal cutouts have been completed and the saw is set up to make the external cut.

◄ Applying white acrylic primer with a small nylon brush.

► The clockface glued in place ready to accept the clock movement.

paper pattern from the decoration guide, and position this over the clock panel, with a sheet of carbon paper between the pattern and panel. Trace over the lines of the pattern with a pencil, leaving an outline on the white surface of the piece. Follow the colouring scheme shown on the example. It doesn't matter if you choose matt or gloss paints, the gloss varnish will add a shiny coat to the finished item. Remember to allow sufficient time for each coat of paint to dry, at least partially, before adding the next colour, otherwise the colours may run.

9 Once all the paint has dried completely, apply a coat of varnish. Coat the edges and front first and lay the panel on top of a tin, or something similar which is smaller than the dial area of the clock while the varnish dries. Then, varnish the back of the panel. Three coats of varnish will be needed to give a good quality finish.

10 Fit the clockface to the clock panel. If the clockface has a protective film over it, leave this in place until after you have finished gluing. It is fairly obvious from the design which way is up, but double check carefully as it will be next to impossible to move the clockface once the glue has begun to harden. Mix up a small amount of two-part epoxy adhesive using a small matchstick. I used a small piece of white card as a mixing palette and a wooden cocktail stick to mix and apply the adhesive to the clockface. Smear a thin film of the adhesive all over the back of the clockface, making sure you have the twelve o'clock in the right position and the dial hole is over the spindle hole.

11 Fit the clock mechanism to-gether using the instructions given by the manufacturer. All you then need to do is fit a battery and your clock is complete.

184mm
(7¼in)

185mm (7¼in)

This template needs to be enlarged by 111%
1 square = 1cm

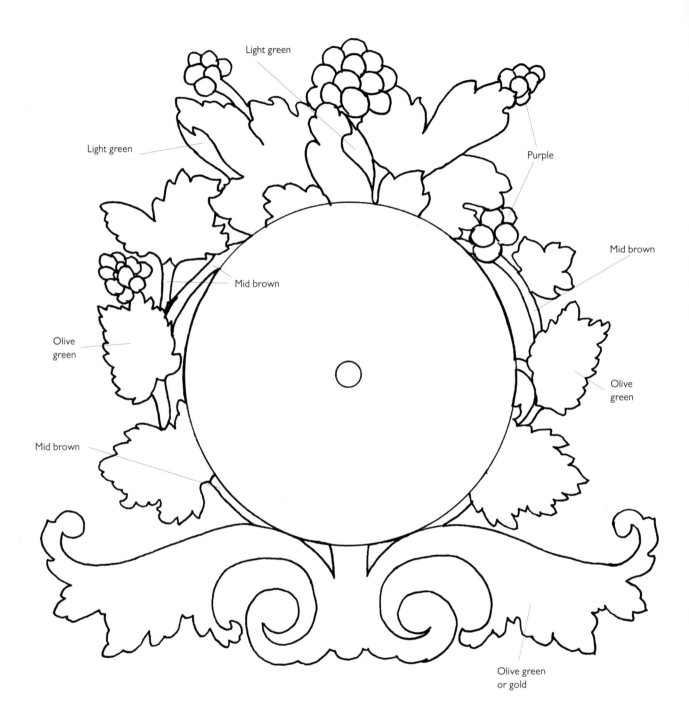

Light green

Light green

Purple

Mid brown

Light green

Olive green

Mid brown

Olive green

Mid brown

Olive green or gold

Decoration guide

Shoe rack

This project offers an answer to having heaps of assorted footwear all over the floor. The shoe rack consists of a pair of end panels, a shoe or boot shelf fixed in place with scroll-cut pegs and a back support brace. The rack can be made almost any length you need by making the shelf and back support brace longer, as the board used for the shelf has ample strength to support a fair number of shoes and boots.

As the end panels and the shelf are relatively large, and cannot be handled easily on the majority of scrollsaws, this project lends itself to the use of a spiral blade. In fact, this is the only option for all but the very largest of scrollsaws, particularly if you want to make a longer shelf than the example shown here. A spiral blade is easy to use once you get used to the fact that you don't have to turn the workpiece to change the direction of the saw cut. It is worth remembering, however, that the tension should be set properly when the blade is fitted. It is also important to avoid using excess pressure against the blade during cutting. The saw's bearings are not designed for sideways pressure, which could prove damaging and dangerous.

EQUIPMENT AND MATERIALS

- 2 pieces of 9mm (³⁄₈in) MDF or plywood, 330mm x 260mm (13in x 10¼in)
- 18mm (¾in) thick pine board
- 1 piece 145mm x 652mm (5¾in x 25¹¹⁄₁₆in)
- 1 piece of the same pine board, 70mm x 600mm (2¾in x 23⁵⁄₈in)
- Offcut of pine board, to make the scroll cut pegs
- 4 round nails, approximately 50mm (2in), to secure the back support brace
- Wood glue
- Decorating materials of your choice

SCROLLSAW BLADE

No. 5 spiral saw blade

TEMPLATES

Back brace	117
Shelf	117
End panel	118
Scroll-cut peg	117

1 Make up a set of cutting patterns. Use the patterns to mark and cut out the blanks. If you are cutting your blanks from sheet material, make use of pre-cut straight edges, where possible, to save scrollsaw cutting time.

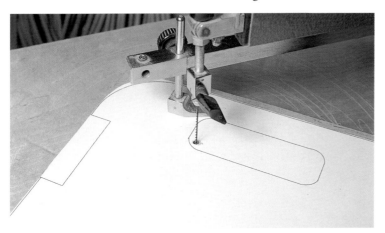

▲ The scrollsaw set up with a spiral blade ready to make the internal cutouts on the end panels.

▶ Rounding off the internal angles of the carrying handle of the end panels for a more comfortable grip.

2 Fix the two end panel blanks together with double-sided adhesive tape and stick the cutting pattern in place on the top blank with spray mount. You will need to make three starter holes in the end panel blanks, one for the carrying handle and one each for the peg joints. Make the internal cutouts first using the spiral blade. Be as accurate as possible when cutting the joints. Once you have completed the internal cutouts, follow round the outside cutting line to complete the end panels.

3 Clean the pieces up with sandpaper making them ready for decoration. Round off the upper edges of the handle cutouts with sandpaper. You can begin

painting the end panels at this point, so they will be completed and ready for final assembly once you have cut out the remaining parts of the project.

4 Stick the cutting patterns on each end of the shelf blank to make the joints. There are two scroll-cut tenon joints at each end of the shelf, each of these has an internal cutout for the peg which locks it in place. Make the starter holes for the internal cutouts in each of the tenons. Thread the spiral blade through the starter hole and check the blade tension. Make sure you cut to the waste side of the cutting line, you can always remove a little material later if the joint is too tight.

5 When you have finished cutting the shelf, check it for fit in the end panels. The joints should be sufficiently tight for the shoe rack to stand up by itself without the back support brace in place. Adjust the fit if it is a little too tight, but be careful not to remove too much material. If the worst happens, you can always cut the tenons off and begin again with a shorter shelf. Check that the end panels are at right angles to the shelf.

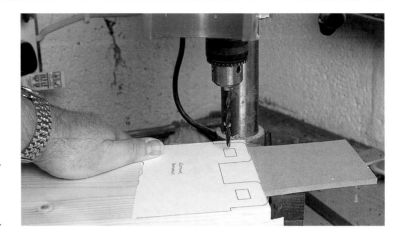

6 You can now check the measurement for the length of the back brace. This brace is just a length of pine, 70mm (2¾in) in width, which stops the shoe rack from rocking when laden with shoes. Cut the brace to length and drill pilot holes for the 50mm (½in) nails.

7 Four scroll-cut pegs are needed to secure the shelf. Lay the cutting pattern for the pegs on an offcut of pine board (the same thickness as the shelf and brace). Cut slightly to the waste side of the cutting line. Test the pegs for fit in the slots you cut in the tenon joints and adjust as necessary. Providing the pegs are a good fit there should be no need for glue to hold everything secure.

▲ Drilling the starter holes for the tenons in the end of the shelf.

◀ Below left Cutting out the pegs.

▼ Below Checking the fit of the shelf and pegs.

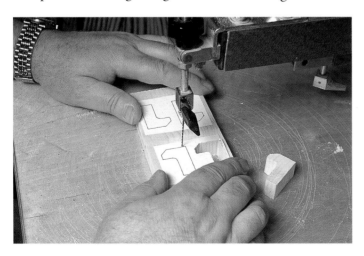

▶ Using a mini-drill to make pilot holes in the end panels, using the holes drilled in the support brace as a guide.

8 Fit the shelf between the end panels and lightly tap in the scroll-cut pegs. Lay the shoe rack face down on the bench and check that the back brace fits. Use a small drill bit to make pilot holes in the end panels. Drill through the holes you have already drilled in the back brace to ensure correct positioning. The use of pilot holes for the nails will prevent the MDF from splitting. Apply a little glue to the end panel where the back support brace fits and nail the brace in place securely. Use a nail punch to drive the nail heads in so that they are flush with the surface of the back brace.

9 Assuming you have already painted the end panels, all that remains is to apply a coat or two of varnish to the finished shoe rack.

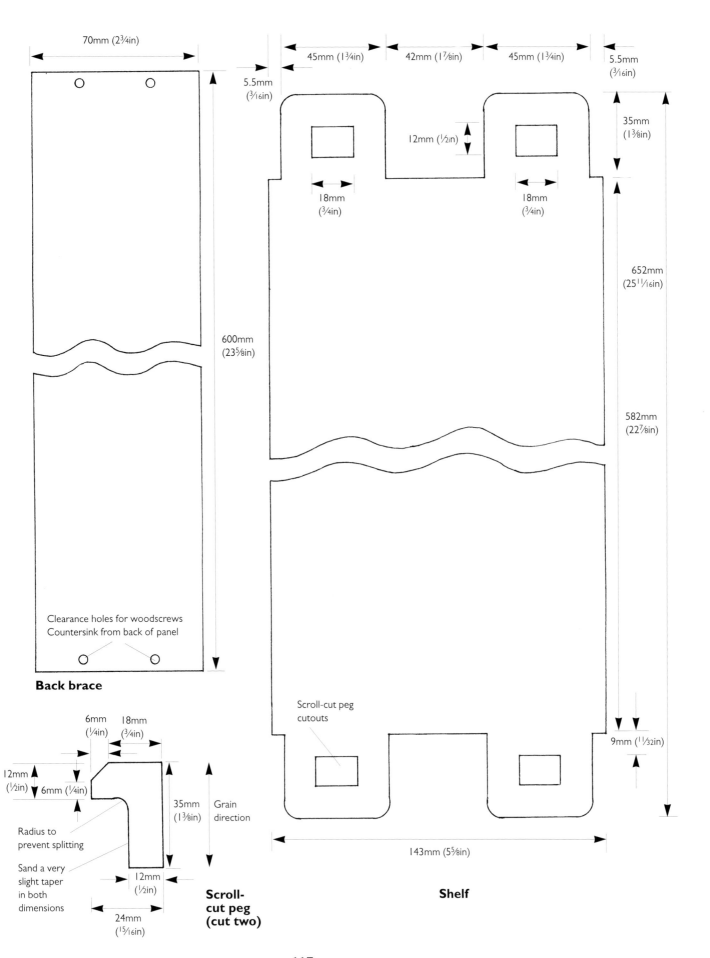

70mm (2¾in)

Back brace

Clearance holes for woodscrews
Countersink from back of panel

600mm
(23⅝in)

5.5mm
(³⁄₁₆in)

45mm (1¾in)

42mm (1⅞in)

45mm (1¾in)

5.5mm
(³⁄₁₆in)

12mm (½in)

18mm
(¾in)

18mm
(¾in)

35mm
(1⅜in)

652mm
(25¹¹⁄₁₆in)

582mm
(22⅞in)

Scroll-cut peg
cutouts

9mm (¹¹⁄₃₂in)

143mm (5⅝in)

Shelf

6mm
(¼in)

18mm
(¾in)

12mm
(½in)

6mm (¼in)

35mm
(1⅜in)

Grain
direction

Radius to
prevent splitting

Sand a very
slight taper
in both
dimensions

12mm
(½in)

24mm
(¹⁵⁄₁₆in)

**Scroll-
cut peg
(cut two)**

117

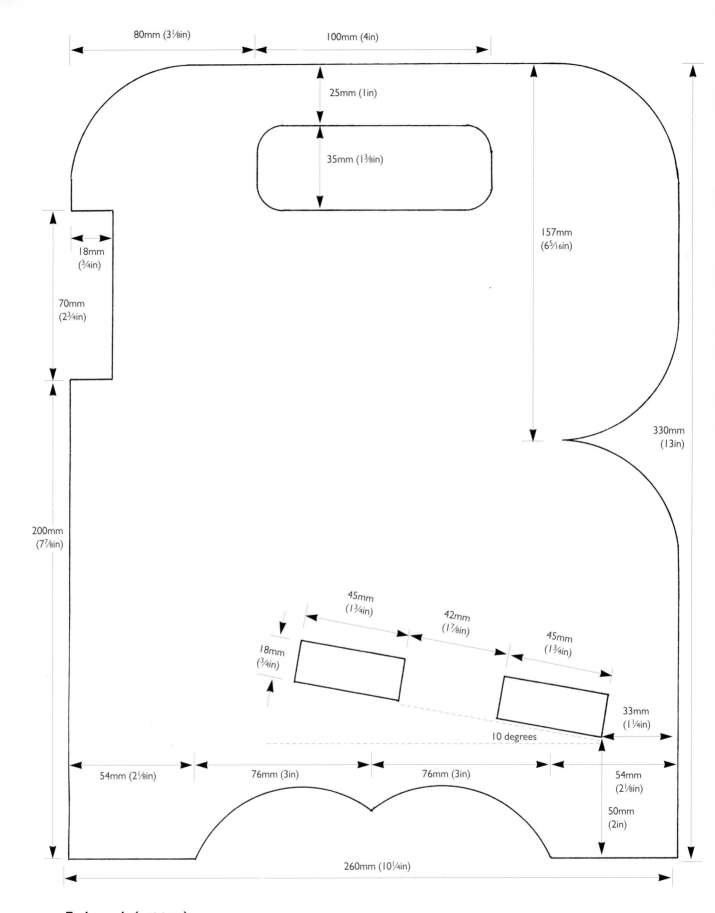

End panels (cut two)

CD rack

This project is a free standing, open-fronted box, with the shelf angled slightly backwards to allow the CDs to sit securely without falling out. The back and side panels have a wavy trellis design cut on the scrollsaw. The shelf is left plain intentionally, as any incised design might snag on the plastic cases of CDs. Only four pieces are needed to make up the complete project.

The rack, which holds about 20 CDs, can be expanded if the dimensions of the example are too small for your CD collection. Just repeat the trellis pattern to create the length of rack you need. Only the length of the shelf and back panel will need to be altered.

The examples shown were made from MDF – 6mm (¼in) thickness for the bottom and back panels, and 9mm (⅜in) thickness for the end panels. Other thicknesses of wood or artificial materials can be used. If you use a different

thickness of material, you will have to adapt the dimensions of the scroll-cut joints on the back panel and shelf. This should not pose any problems, providing you make sure there will be a long enough length of tenon to fit the slot in the end panels.

EQUIPMENT AND MATERIALS

- 2 pieces of 9mm (⅜in) MDF, 170mm x 150mm (6¾in x 6in), for the end panels
- 1 piece of 6mm (¼in) MDF, 280mm x 140mm (11in x 5½in), for the shelf
- 1 piece of 6mm (¼in) MDF, 280mm x 130mm (11in x 5⅛in), for the back panel
- Paint or your choice of decoration
- Wood glue

SCROLLSAW BLADE

No. 7 skip-tooth scroll saw blade (if you use MDF)

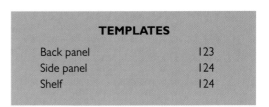

TEMPLATES	
Back panel	123
Side panel	124
Shelf	124

1 Decide whether you want to make the CD rack according to the sizes given, or if you wish to make it longer. Make up the cutting patterns according to your own requirements.

2 Try to make blanks for the side panels, shelf and back panels along the pre-cut edges of the sheet of MDF, as this will save you making an additional cut. The two side panel blanks can be made into a stack and cut out together. Using a few pieces of double-sided adhesive tape on the waste side of the cutting line, attach the blanks together. Drill the starter holes in the positions indicated on the templates. The positions given for the starter holes make the job easier to clean up afterwards.

3 Cut out the four pieces, making the internal cutouts first. Cut out the four pieces in no special order. If you are making a longer version of the CD rack and have a limited throat capacity on your scrollsaw, use a spiral blade as mentioned earlier. You can also cut out the side panels with the spiral blade if you wish to avoid changing blades.

▲ Drilling out the starter holes.

► Drilling the starter holes for the back panel in the same positions as for the end panels.

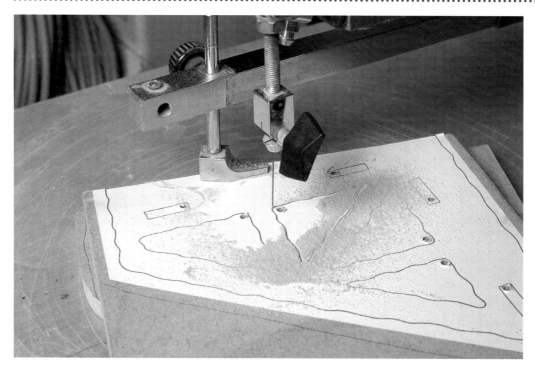

◀ Nearing completion of the first internal cut. The starter hole position which will ensure a neat finish.

▲ Trying out the fit of the panels prior to gluing.

▲ Filing the scallop edge on the end panel with a round file.

4 When you have cut out the four pieces for the CD rack, clean up any saw tearout with fine sandpaper and check the pieces fit together. Make any slight adjustments as needed.

5 Scallop the edges of the side panels with a half-round file. About three good strokes of the file in the indentations around the edges of the trellis lines should be adequate.

► The assembled rack with a couple of G cramps holding the back and bottom panels together while the adhesive sets.

6 Apply a little wood glue to the joint ends of the shelf and back panels as well as along the lower edge of the back panel where it will fit to the shelf. Fit the parts together and clamp in place until the glue is dry.

7 When the glue has set, sand where and if necessary to ensure a clean finish, particularly where the joints of the bottom and back panels pass through the side panels. Use a little wood filler if needed around the joints and sand smooth when it has set.

8 Decoration is a matter of personal choice. There are many ways in which you can finish off your CD rack. It may be that you want to paint it to fit in with a room decor, or you may want to go for a more ornate approach and complete it with the artificial gold leaf (obtainable from most good craft shops). Coloured varnishes are another option. I used a stone fleck finish which is available from DIY stores in an aerosol can. The stone fleck effect is just a plastic coating and not actual stone and will not damage CDs.

Back panel

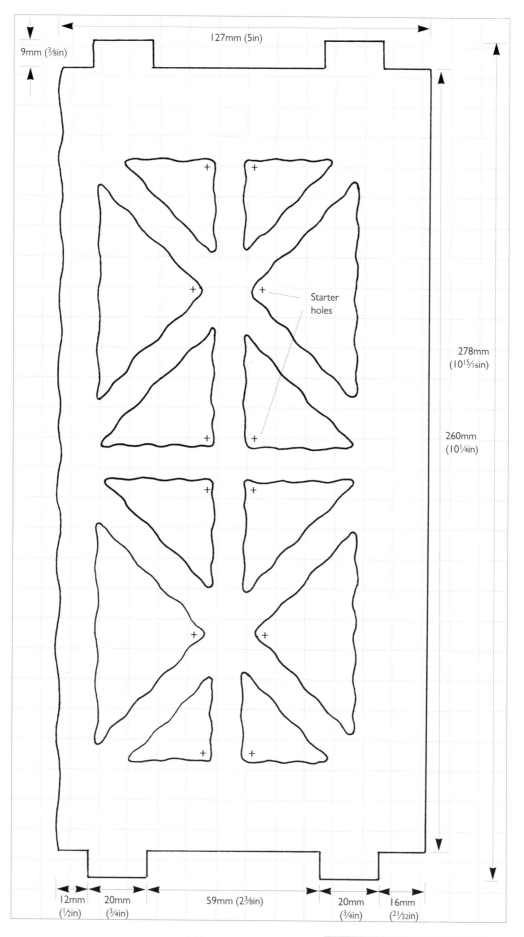

127mm (5in)

9mm (³⁄₈in)

Starter holes

278mm (10¹⁵⁄₁₆in)

260mm (10¹⁄₄in)

12mm (¹⁄₂in)

20mm (³⁄₄in)

59mm (2³⁄₈in)

20mm (³⁄₄in)

16mm (²¹⁄₃₂in)

123

This template needs to be enlarged by 125%
1 square = 1cm

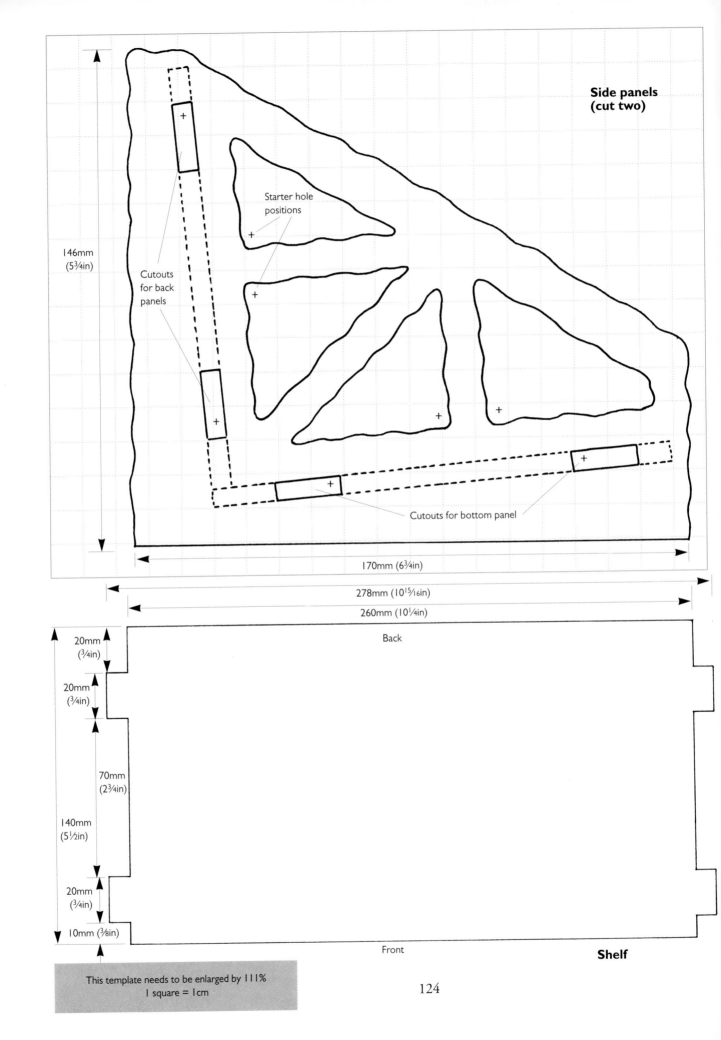

**Side panels
(cut two)**

146mm
(5¾in)

Starter hole
positions

Cutouts
for back
panels

Cutouts for bottom panel

170mm (6¾in)

278mm (10¹⁵⁄₁₆in)

260mm (10¼in)

Back

20mm
(¾in)

20mm
(¾in)

70mm
(2¾in)

140mm
(5½in)

20mm
(¾in)

10mm (³⁄₈in)

Front

Shelf

This template needs to be enlarged by 111%
1 square = 1cm

124

Ring and necklace rack

This earring rack and ring tray has an upright scrolled panel for drop earrings and four trays built into the base, for stud earrings and rings. There are three main parts involved in the construction of this project – the upright panel and upper and lower bases. The upper base has cutouts which form trays for rings and stud earrings, while the lower base forms the bottom of the unit.

The example shown was made from a small sheet of 6mm (¼in) mahogany (a remnant from a Georgian dresser). If you don't happen to have a sheet of mahogany to hand, don't worry. With suitable decoration, this project can look every bit as good if made from MDF, oak and most other woods. MDF will need more decoration than natural wood. Material much thicker than the 6mm (¼in) specified will make the finished project look rather chunky.

This is one of those projects where you will need to follow the sequence of operations closely to succeed.

EQUIPMENT AND MATERIALS

Sheet material of your choice, mahogany was used for the example

- 1 piece about 120mm x 190mm (4¾in x 7½in), for the upright panel
- 2 pieces of a little over 200mm (7⅞in) square, for the two bases
- 3 woodscrews No. 4 15mm(⅝in)
- Wood glue, for mounting the upright panel
- Drill bits, to drill pilot and clearance holes for woodscrews, see chart on page 8

- Double-sided adhesive tape
- Spray mount
- Decorating materials of your choice. (The only decoration applied to the example, being natural wood, was a little furniture polish and a clean cloth.)
- Square of felt, for underneath the base, to prevent the piece from scratching a highly polished surface (optional)

SCROLLSAW BLADE
No. 7 skip-tooth blade, if you are using MDF
No. 7 general purpose blade, for solid wood
material

TEMPLATES	
Base	130
Upright panel	131

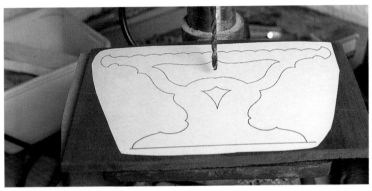

▲ Drilling the starter holes in the upright panel.

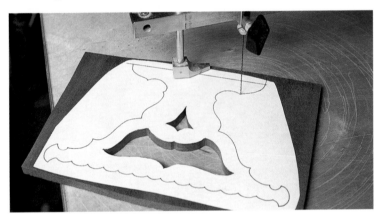

▲ Making the external cut on the upright panel once the internal cutouts are complete.

▲ Drilling the starter holes in the top base blank.

1 Make up the cutting patterns. There will be two in this instance, one for the upright panel and one for the base. Although there are two base pieces, only one cutting pattern, containing all the information for cutting both pieces, is needed. Mark out the blanks for the three pieces on the sheet material. Cut the blanks and spray mount the cutting patterns in place on the panel blank and one of the base blanks.

2 Drill the starter holes for the two internal cutouts on the upright panel. Thread the appropriate blade through each of these in turn, and make the internal cutouts. Remember, if you are using sheet wood for this project, the blade will cut much faster across the grain and so extra care will be needed to maintain an accurate cut. Keep careful control of your workpiece and you should not have any problems.

3 Carry out the external cut on the upright panel, making sure that the bottom edge is even. Remove what is left of the cutting pattern and gently clean up any saw tearout with fine sandpaper. Check the straight edge with a steel ruler and sand down if necessary. Put this part to one side for the moment.

4 Take the base blank with the cutting pattern attached and drill starter holes for the four internal cutouts. These are best drilled close to the middle of the blank, making cleaning up afterwards more uniform, and avoiding the possibility of uneven ellipses on the four cutouts. Make the four internal cutouts.

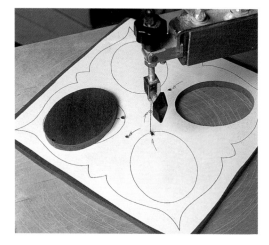

◄ Making the internal cutouts which will form the ring trays in the top base panel.

5 Clean any saw tearout out of the ring tray ellipses. I used a small drum sander fitted in a bench drill. If you do not have a drum sander, glue sandpaper around a cylinder of any reasonable diameter, such as a broom handle, this should work just as well.

◄ Sanding the completed upper base with a drum sander to even out the ellipses of the ring trays.

▼ Using double-sided adhesive tape to secure the upper and bottom bases together prior to making the external cut.

6 Take the upper base with the internal cutouts completed and, with a few small pieces of double-sided adhesive tape, attach it to the remaining base blank to create a stack. Set up your scrollsaw to accommodate the stack and make the external cut. This not only saves time, but also means that both pieces are identical. Once you have completed this cut, clean up both pieces with fine sandpaper.

▶ Making the external cut in the two bases. Note the cut begins at a sharp point which will make cleaning up afterwards much simpler.

▼ Marking the position for the pilot holes in the upright panel.

▲ Screwing the upright panel in place on the upper base.

7 Remove the cutting pattern from the bases and mark out the fixing holes for the upright panel in the upper base (see template for exact positions). Drill clearance holes for the No. 4 woodscrews in the base. Countersink the holes from underneath the panel and sand off if needed. Mark out the positions for the pilot holes in the upright panel with a sharp pencil. Drill pilot holes in the upright panels.

8 Add a small amount of wood glue along the bottom edge of the upright panel, taking care not to use so much that it will spread out from the join when the screws are done up. Insert and tighten the three woodscrews, making sure they sit flush with the underside of the upper base or they will make fitting the bottom base almost impossible. Allow sufficient time for the glue to harden before continuing.

9 Glue the bottom base to the top base. Make certain you have the two panels matched up correctly so that the edges line up neatly. A smear of wood glue applied to the underside of the top base is all that is necessary. Be careful that no glue spreads out over the ring trays. Clamp the two parts together to dry.

10 Once the glue has set completely, carry out any decoration you wish in order to complete the piece.

▲ The two bases joined and clamped while the glue sets.

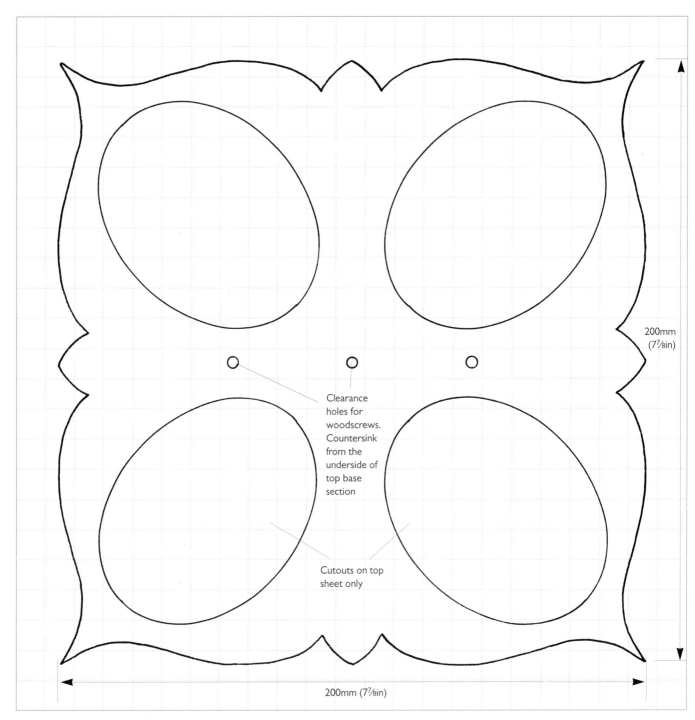

200mm
(7⅞in)

Clearance
holes for
woodscrews.
Countersink
from the
underside of
top base
section

Cutouts on top
sheet only

200mm (7⅞in)

Base

130

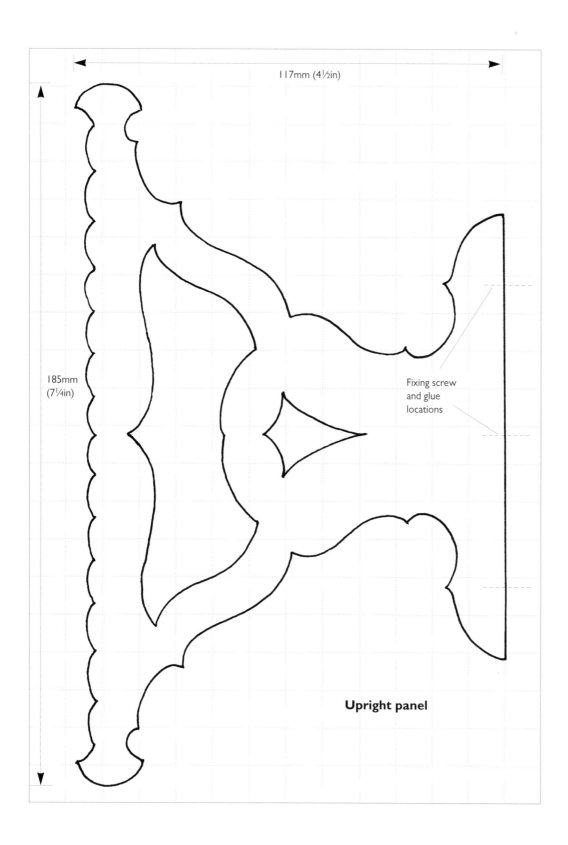

117mm (4½in)

185mm
(7¼in)

Fixing screw
and glue
locations

Upright panel

131

This template is actual size
1 square = 1cm

Tool caddy

This tool caddy is sturdy and has one or two refinements which make it ideally suited to construction with the scrollsaw. The basic box section has a central dividing panel, which also acts as a handle, locked in place with a scroll-cut projection at each end. This makes the caddy much stronger. The lower portion of the slot of the carrying handle is reproduced on each of the side panels. This helps to avoid scraped knuckles when you pick up the caddy.

An optional feature of this caddy is the title, which is scroll cut into one or both of the side panels. A further refinement could be the addition of the owner's name.

EQUIPMENT AND MATERIALS

9mm (³⁄₈in) MDF

- 1 piece measuring 350mm x 180mm (13¹³⁄₁₆in x 7in), for the centre panel
- 1 piece measuring 340mm x 275mm (13³⁄₈in x 10¹³⁄₁₆in), for the bottom panel

18mm (³⁄₄in) pine board

- 2 pieces measuring 350mm x 145mm (13¹³⁄₁₆in x 5¾in), for the side panels
- 2 pieces 275mm x 145mm (10¹³⁄₁₆in x 5¾in),

for the end panels
- 8 mirror screws No. 8 32mm (1¼in)
- 16 woodscrews No. 8 32mm (1¼in)
- 2 woodscrews No. 6 24mm (²⁹⁄₃₂in)
- Drill bits, to drill pilot and clearance holes for woodscrews, see chart on page 8
- Wood glue
- Two-part epoxy resin
- Paint, for decoration

SCROLLSAW BLADE

No. 5 skip-tooth blade
If your saw has a large throat capacity, you can use this blade for all the cuts on this project, but if you have a smaller machine and wish to add the lettering to the side panel use a spiral blade.

TEMPLATES

Central panel	137
Bottom panel	138
End panel	139
Side panel	140

1 Make up a set of cutting patterns. You will need two copies each of the end panel and side panel patterns. Either follow the measurements given, or adapt the dimensions to your own requirements. Make up blanks for all pieces.

2 Stick the centre panel cutting pattern on the appropriate MDF blank. When cutting out the blank, take advantage of any pre-cut straight edges. Drill a starter hole for the carrying handle cutout. Make the cutout with the skip-tooth blade, then make the external cut. Clean up the piece with sandpaper, especially inside the handle, and apply a coat of primer, followed by a couple of coats in the colour of your choice. Put the panel aside until the paint dries.

3 Fit a general purpose blade to the scrollsaw and cut out the two end panels from pine board. Pay particular attention to the recess in the centre of the panel which needs to fit closely with the projection of the centre panel. This part will carry most of the weight of the full caddy when it is being carried around.

4 The side panels are similar to the end panels with one or two additional features. Decide at this point if you wish to incorporate the tool caddy lettering (or any other customizing feature) and make the relevant starter holes in the design. The scroll-cut tenon

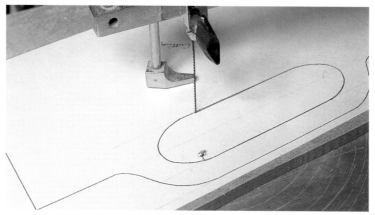

▲ The centre panel set up on the scrollsaw with the internal cutout almost completed.

▲ Rounding off the hard edges of the carrying handle.

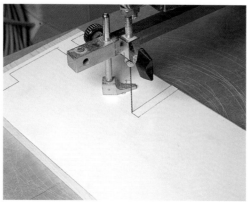

◄ The end panel set up on the saw with the slot for the centre panel being cut out.

► Making the internal cutouts within the letters.

joints on the side panels fix into the end panels, so that they project a little. This is purely for decorative effect, cut them flush if you prefer. Make the external cut to both side panels.

5 If you intend to add lettering and your scrollsaw has a limited throat capacity, fit a spiral blade and make the appropriate cutouts. Smooth off the lettering using a round file.

▲ The completed lettering panel.

► Cleaning up the internal parts of the letters with a fine file. Sandpaper is a little too awkward to use for this job.

◄ Testing the panels for fit. Adjust where needed at this point before any final assembly is attempted.

▼ Marking either side of the centre panel with the top of the tool caddy assembled to ensure the securing screws, which fasten the bottom panel to the centre panel, will lie dead centre of the MDF board to prevent splitting.

6 Try putting together all of the panels you have made so far and check that they fit together easily. If the fit is too tight, the tenons can be filed or gently pared with a wood chisel.

7 When you are happy with the fit of the panels, check the dimensions of the cutting pattern of the bottom panel by laying the side, end and centre panels fitted together, in place over the cutting pattern. Draw a pencil line down each side of the centre panel onto the cutting pattern. This will help you to mark the exact positions of the clearance holes in the bottom piece. Cut out the bottom panel from MDF, again making use of any pre-cut straight edges.

8 Drill clearance holes, as marked, in the side and bottom panels.

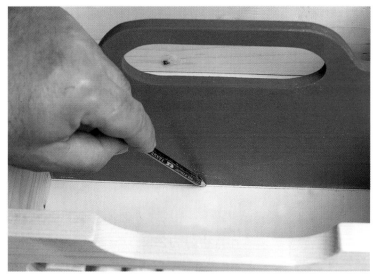

9 Check that all the pieces fit together properly. Begin assembly by slotting the two end panels in place over the projections at each end of the centre panel. Add wood glue to the joints where the wood surfaces meet.

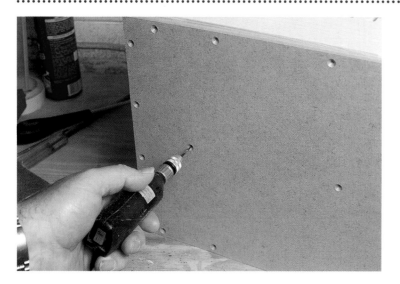

▲ Using a mini-drill to make pilot holes in the centre panel through the clearance holes drilled in the bottom board. This prevents the MDF from splitting when the fixing screws are inserted and tightened.

10 Fit the side panels to the end panels, again adding wood glue where the side and end pieces meet. Do up the mirror screws, but leave the cover caps until later.

11 Turn the fitted pieces upside down and support them on two lengths of 50mm (2in) square timber, allowing the carrying handle to clear the bench. Smear wood glue around the underside of all the panels. Screw the bottom panel onto the side and end panels. Use a small drill bit to make pilot holes in the bottom of the centre panel so that the screws do not split the MDF. Fit the remaining screws.

12 Mix up some two-part epoxy glue to fit the mirror screw caps. Smear some over each of the mirror cover caps and attach them over the screws in the side panels. When the glue has completely dried, varnish or stain the completed caddy to your own preferences.

► The finished tool caddy with the cover caps of the mirror screws in place.

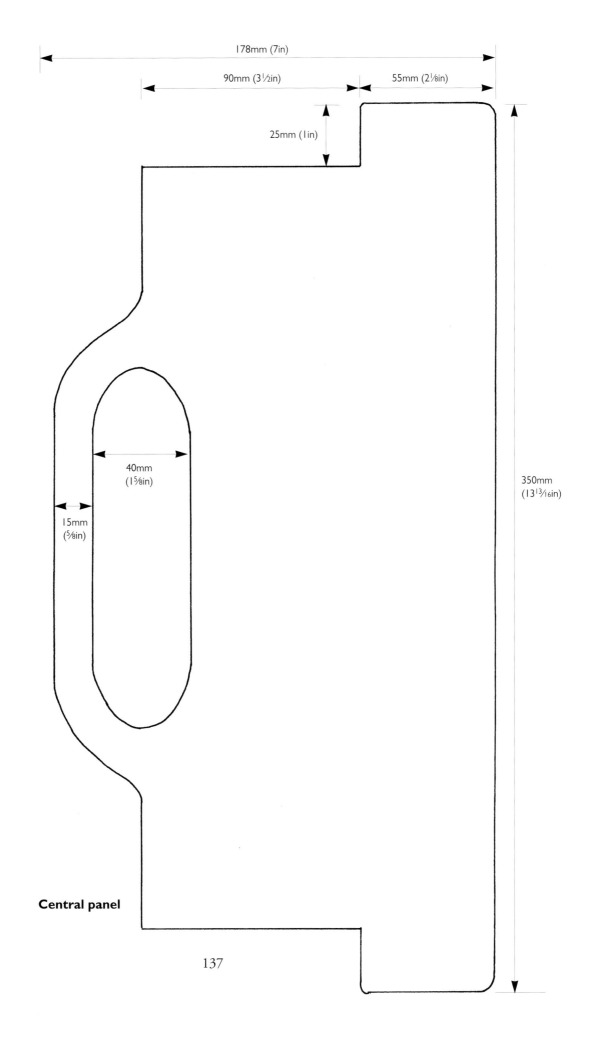

178mm (7in)

90mm (3½in)

55mm (2⅛in)

25mm (1in)

40mm
(1⅝in)

15mm
(⅝in)

350mm
(13¹³/₁₆in)

Central panel

137

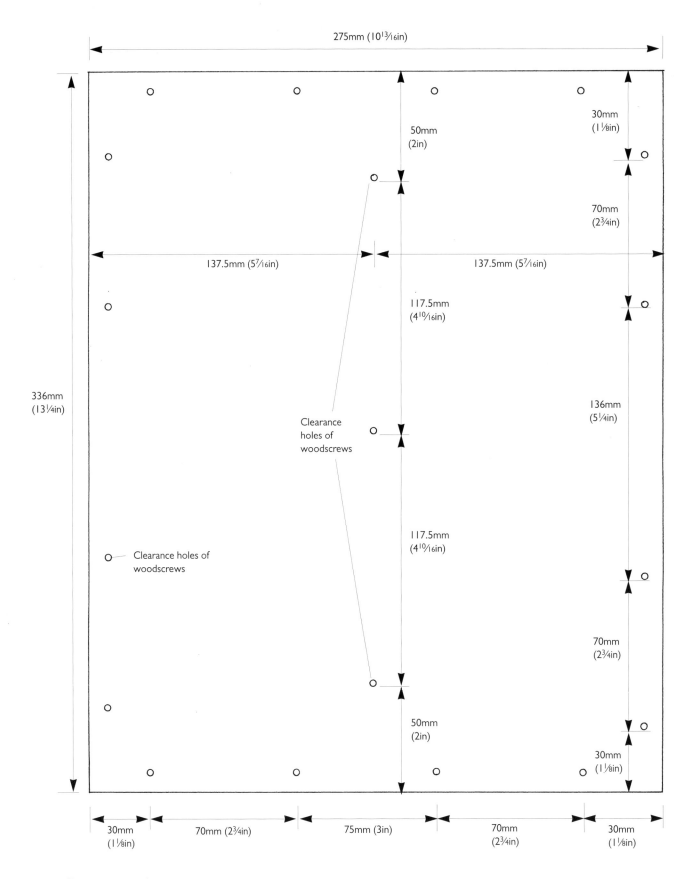

275mm (10¹³/₁₆in)

30mm (1⅛in)

50mm (2in)

70mm (2¾in)

137.5mm (5⁷/₁₆in)   137.5mm (5⁷/₁₆in)

117.5mm (4¹⁰/₁₆in)

336mm (13¼in)

136mm (5¼in)

Clearance holes of woodscrews

117.5mm (4¹⁰/₁₆in)

Clearance holes of woodscrews

70mm (2¾in)

50mm (2in)

30mm (1⅛in)

30mm (1⅛in)   70mm (2¾in)   75mm (3in)   70mm (2¾in)   30mm (1⅛in)

Bottom panel

**End panels
(cut two)**

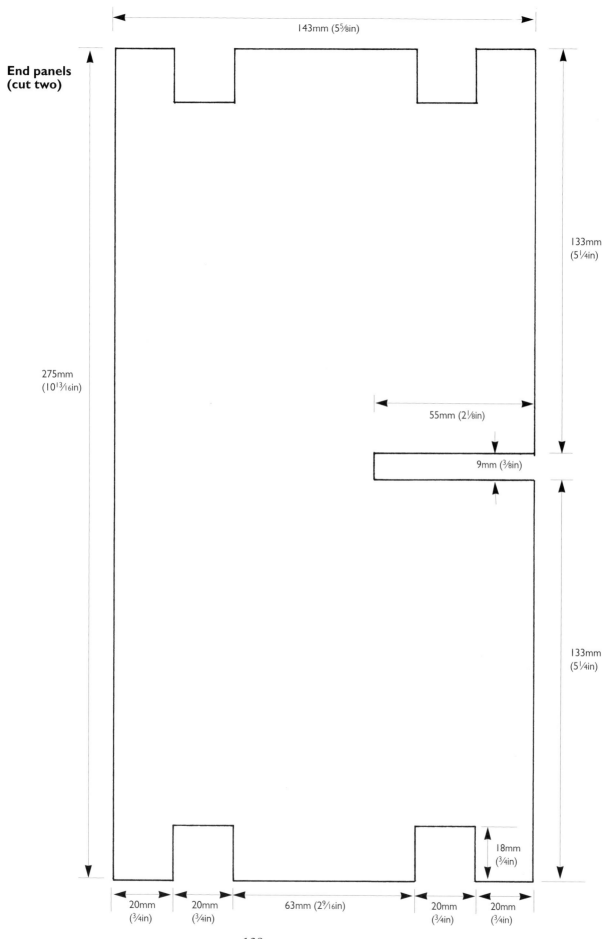

143mm (5⅝in)

133mm
(5¼in)

275mm
(10¹³⁄₁₆in)

55mm (2⅛in)

9mm (⅜in)

133mm
(5¼in)

18mm
(¾in)

20mm
(¾in)

20mm
(¾in)

63mm (2⁹⁄₁₆in)

20mm
(¾in)

20mm
(¾in)

20mm (¾in)   20mm (¾in)   143mm (5⅝in)   20mm (¾in)   20mm (¾in)

63mm (2½in)

**Side panels
(cut two)**

25mm (1in)

350mm (13¹³⁄₁₆in)

TOOL CADDY

Clearance holes for woodscrews

25mm (1in)

140

This template needs to be enlarged by 153%
1 square = 1.5cm

PROJECT 20

Wind vane

T his wind vane is constructed largely from offcuts and scrap materials and so costs little, if anything, to make. The essence of this project is to make do with whatever might be available to you rather than buying timber especially for the project. The wooden parts are fairly straightforward and the swivel is made from a defunct castor wheel.

The wind vane only uses a short length of timber as a support, so would be perfect for mounting on a garden shed, but there is no reason why the support shouldn't be as long as required. You could even utilize a redundant television antenna pole by ramming a short length of timber into its top to take the socket part of the castor.

EQUIPMENT AND MATERIALS

- 1 castor and swivel socket
- A few short lengths of 12mm (½in) dowel
- A few small pieces of 3-6mm (⅛–¼in) sheet material, for the letters and arrow parts
- A thicker piece of timber for the arrow mounting block. (The thickness of this will depend on the castor you intend to use. The one used here was 20mm (¾in) thick.)
- A length of 50mm (2in) square timber for the support post

- A flat file and thin punch, to remove the wheel and axle from the old castor
- Wood bit, 12mm (¼in)
- Drill bit, to suit the centre hole of the castor frame which will take the fixing bolt and nut
- Nut and bolt, to suit the frame hole of the castor
- Wood glue
- Decorating materials and varnish

► Filing away the burred over metal on the castor, to allow the axle to be punched clear.

▼ The castor and socket pieces separated out from each other.

1 Remove the swivel socket of the castor and put to one side. This may need to be levered off with a flat screwdriver. File away the burred over metal which holds the axle of the castor, then punch out the axle. The axle and wheel can be discarded.

2 Measure the distance between the side flanges of the castor frame. This will give you the required thickness of the centre piece of timber which will carry the arrow. On the example shown, the measurement was 20mm (¾in). Locate a suitable small piece of timber of a suitable thickness, refer to the arrow mounting block template for further dimensions. Attach the cutting pattern to the offcut of

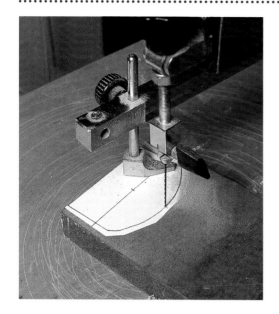

wood and cut it to shape on the scrollsaw and sand smooth. Using the 12mm (¼in) wood bit drill, the hole through the piece as shown in the template. If you find it difficult to hold this piece of wood, you can make up a simple jig, from two square offcuts of timber, to hold it in place. This should keep it steady enough to allow you to make a fairly straight hole through the centre of the piece of wood.

3 Cut a 280mm (11in) length of dowel for the arrow. Make the arrow as long or as short as you like, but remember it must be long enough for the wind to turn it. Cut a slot in each end of the dowel to take the arrow parts. This can easily be done on the scrollsaw. It helps to make the two straight cuts into the ends of the dowel first before completing the cut by turning the dowel

◄ *Above left* Cutting out the arrow mounting block on the scrollsaw.

▲ *Above*
A makeshift jig for holding the centre block for drilling.

◄ Cutting the dowel slots on the scrollsaw. Make sure while doing this operation that the dowel remains vertical during cutting.

▶ Setting up the drill to make the fixing hole for the bolt and nut.

at right angles to make the final cut. Make sure you cut the slot to the thickness of the material you are using for the arrow parts, 6mm (¼in) in this case.

4 Insert the dowel into the arrow mounting block and, using the side flanges of the castor as a guide, mark a hole for the fixing bolt and nut. Make sure that the slots in the ends of the dowel

▼ Cutting out the letter and arrow parts on the scrollsaw.

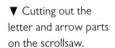

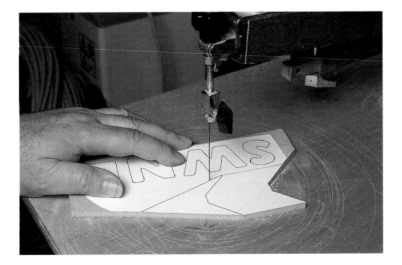

are vertical before you drill. Using an appropriate size drill bit, drill through the arrow mounting block and the dowel. Apply a little wood glue to the dowel before finally fitting it in the mounting block. Do not try to force the castor in place. If it is a little tight, remove some wood from the arrow mounting block with sandpaper until you have a snug fit. Fit the castor in place with the fixing bolt and nut.

5 Make up a cutting pattern for the letters and arrow parts in the sizes indicated and attach it to the sheet material you intend to use. Set up your scrollsaw and cut out the letters and arrow parts. Clean up any saw tearout with sandpaper. Check that the arrow parts slot in place in the cut dowel rod. Glue the parts in place and put the piece aside for the moment to allow the glue to set thoroughly.

6 Take the length of 50mm (2in) square timber and mark the central point in one end of it. Draw two diagonal lines from corner to corner. The inter-section of these two lines will mark the central point. Select a drill bit which will make a clearance hole for the castor socket. Lay the castor socket alongside the drill bit and mark the depth needed on the drill bit by winding a piece of tape around the bit at the depth you want. Drill the hole with an appro-priate size drill bit.

7 Mark out and drill the 12mm (½in) holes for the direction indicator dowels (positions are marked on the template). These will need to be in the centre of each side of the timber, a little way below the depth of the castor hole. Make one hole as close to the bottom of the castor socket as you can, and the other hole, which will be at right angles to the first, slightly lower down. Drill these holes with the 12mm (½in) wood bit. Fit the castor socket. The most

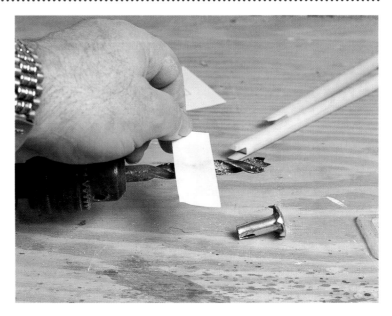

▲ Marking the drill bit for depth prior to drilling the castor socket hole.

common type, such as the one used here, has a grip around the top of the socket so that it can be hammered into the timber and will stay there with no further fixing necessary.

8 Cut two lengths of 280mm (11in) of 12mm (½in) dowel for the direction letters. Cut slots in both ends of each dowel length to fit the letters as before. Angle the bottom of the slots

◀ Testing to see if the lettering fits in the dowel rod slots.

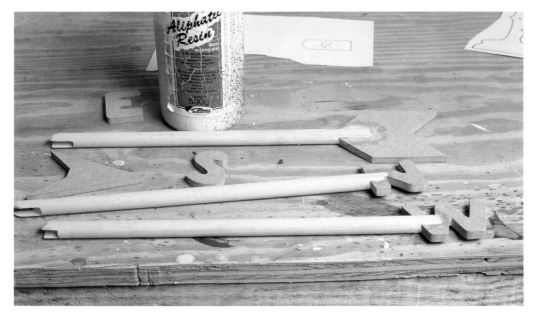

► Tapping the castor socket into place.

▼ The assembled and painted wind vane ready for installation.

which will take the S and W, as the letters curve and a matching angle in the slot will add strength to the finished item. You can either do this on the scrollsaw, or just file the angle after cutting the slot. Check the size of the slots by inserting the letters.

9 Glue the dowels centrally through the holes in the support post and leave for the glue to set. Glue the letters into the slots, making sure they are in the right positions or the final result will have the compass points in the wrong places.

10 Decorate the wind vane to your own preferences. I used Humbrol enamel paints coated with yachting varnish to make it more weatherproof. Once the decoration is dry, slot the arrow into place. The arrow should swing freely in the wind but can be eased with a file if it tends to stick a little.

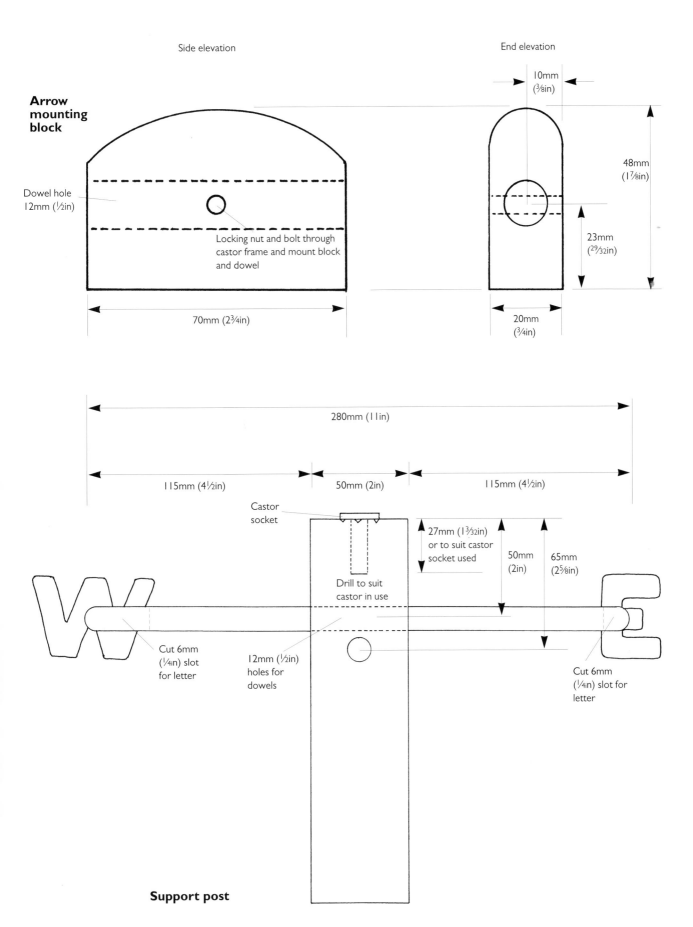

Side elevation

End elevation

Arrow mounting block

Dowel hole 12mm (½in)

Locking nut and bolt through castor frame and mount block and dowel

10mm (⅜in)

48mm (1⅞in)

23mm (²⁹⁄₃₂in)

70mm (2¾in)

20mm (¾in)

280mm (11in)

115mm (4½in)

50mm (2in)

115mm (4½in)

Castor socket

27mm (1³⁄₃₂in) or to suit castor socket used

50mm (2in)

65mm (2⅝in)

Drill to suit castor in use

Cut 6mm (¼in) slot for letter

12mm (½in) holes for dowels

Cut 6mm (¼in) slot for letter

Support post

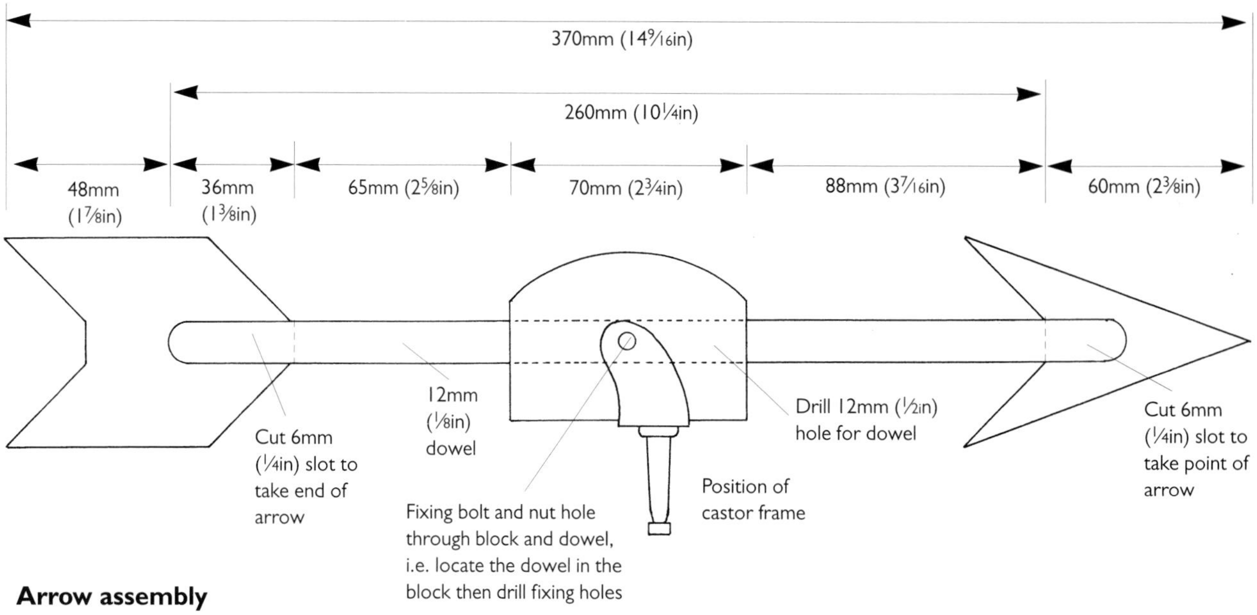
370mm ($14\frac{9}{16}$in)
260mm ($10\frac{1}{4}$in)
48mm ($1\frac{7}{8}$in)
36mm ($1\frac{3}{8}$in)
65mm ($2\frac{5}{8}$in)
70mm ($2\frac{3}{4}$in)
88mm ($3\frac{7}{16}$in)
60mm ($2\frac{3}{8}$in)
Cut 6mm ($\frac{1}{4}$in) slot to take end of arrow
12mm ($\frac{1}{8}$in) dowel
Fixing bolt and nut hole through block and dowel, i.e. locate the dowel in the block then drill fixing holes
Position of castor frame
Drill 12mm ($\frac{1}{2}$in) hole for dowel
Cut 6mm ($\frac{1}{4}$in) slot to take point of arrow

Arrow assembly

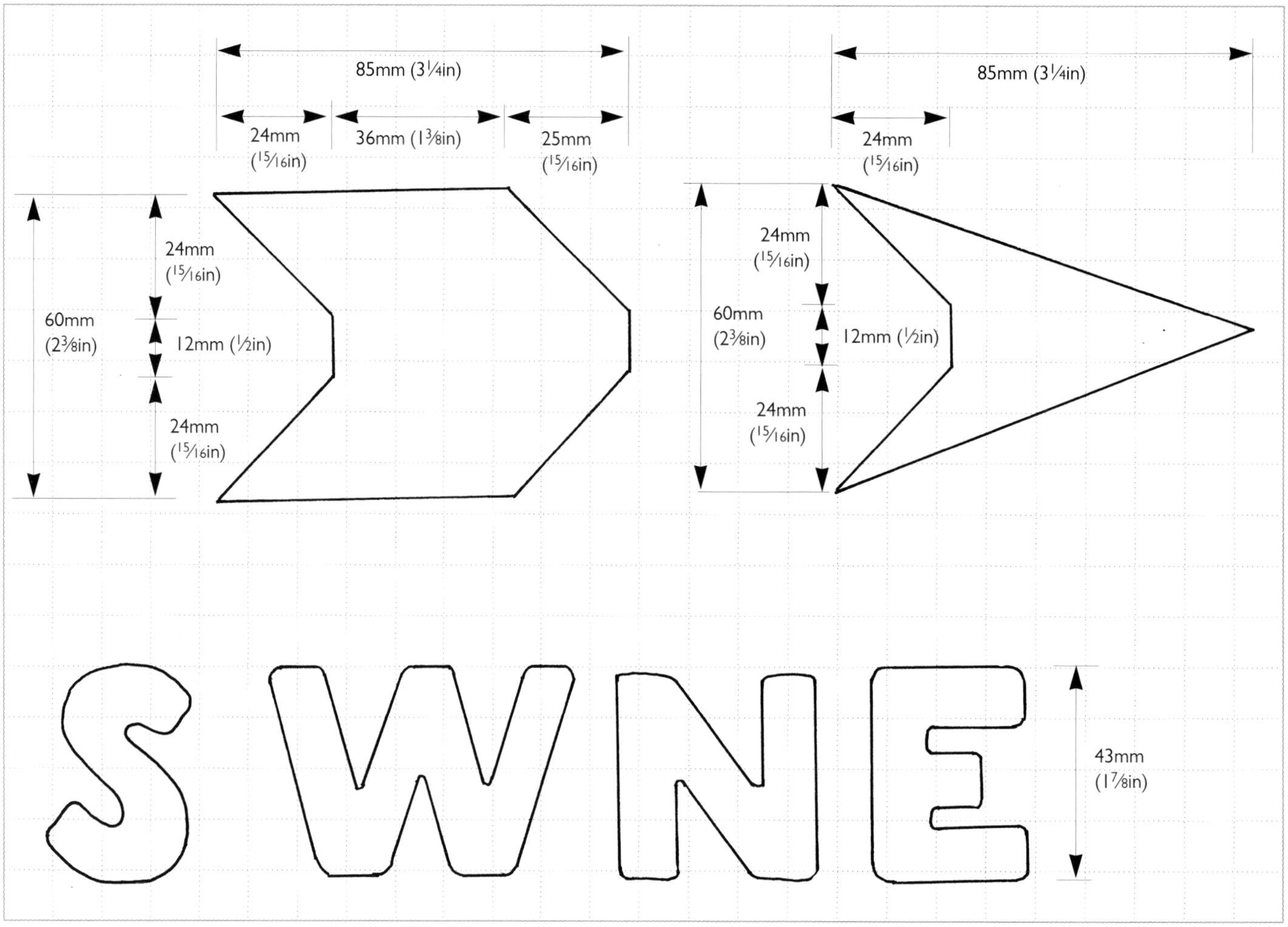
85mm ($3\frac{1}{4}$in)
24mm ($\frac{15}{16}$in)
36mm ($1\frac{3}{8}$in)
25mm ($\frac{15}{16}$in)
85mm ($3\frac{1}{4}$in)
24mm ($\frac{15}{16}$in)
60mm ($2\frac{3}{8}$in)
24mm ($\frac{15}{16}$in)
12mm ($\frac{1}{2}$in)
24mm ($\frac{15}{16}$in)
60mm ($2\frac{3}{8}$in)
24mm ($\frac{15}{16}$in)
12mm ($\frac{1}{2}$in)
24mm ($\frac{15}{16}$in)
SWNE
43mm ($1\frac{7}{8}$in)

Indicator parts

This template needs to be enlarged by 140%
1 square = 1cm

About the author

John Everett is a technical artist and photographer. He has a long-standing interest in woodwork, and is a keen scrollsaw enthusiast.

He lives in Wales, where he has a workshop. He produces craft kits and projects for a range of individuals and organisations including schools and colleges.

Index

BOOKS

WOODCARVING

The Art of the Woodcarver	GMC Publications
Carving Birds & Beasts	GMC Publications
Carving on Turning	Chris Pye
Carving Realistic Birds	David Tippey
Decorative Woodcarving	Jeremy Williams
Essential Tips for Woodcarvers	GMC Publications
Essential Woodcarving Techniques	Dick Onians
Lettercarving in Wood: A Practical Course	Chris Pye
Power Tools for Woodcarving	David Tippey
Practical Tips for Turners & Carvers	GMC Publications
Relief Carving in Wood: A Practical Introduction	Chris Pye
Understanding Woodcarving	GMC Publications
Understanding Woodcarving in the Round	GMC Publications
Useful Techniques for Woodcarvers	GMC Publications
Wildfowl Carving – Volume 1	Jim Pearce
Wildfowl Carving – Volume 2	Jim Pearce
The Woodcarvers	GMC Publications
Woodcarving: A Complete Course	Ron Butterfield
Woodcarving: A Foundation Course	Zoë Gertner
Woodcarving for Beginners	GMC Publications
Woodcarving Tools & Equipment Test Reports	GMC Publications
Woodcarving Tools, Materials & Equipment	Chris Pye

WOODTURNING

Adventures in Woodturning	David Springett
Bert Marsh: Woodturner	Bert Marsh
Bill Jones' Notes from the Turning Shop	Bill Jones
Bill Jones' Further Notes from the Turning Shop	Bill Jones
Colouring Techniques for Woodturners	Jan Sanders
The Craftsman Woodturner	Peter Child
Decorative Techniques for Woodturners	Hilary Bowen
Essential Tips for Woodturners	GMC Publications
Faceplate Turning	GMC Publications
Fun at the Lathe	R.C. Bell
Illustrated Woodturning Techniques	John Hunnex
Intermediate Woodturning Projects	GMC Publications
Keith Rowley's Woodturning Projects	Keith Rowley
Make Money from Woodturning	Ann & Bob Phillips
Multi-Centre Woodturning	Ray Hopper
Pleasure and Profit from Woodturning	Reg Sherwin
Practical Tips for Turners & Carvers	GMC Publications
Practical Tips for Woodturners	GMC Publications
Spindle Turning	GMC Publications
Turning Miniatures in Wood	John Sainsbury
Turning Wooden Toys	Terry Lawrence
Understanding Woodturning	Ann & Bob Phillips
Useful Techniques for Woodturners	GMC Publications
Useful Woodturning Projects	GMC Publications
Woodturning: Bowls, Platters, Hollow Forms, Vases, Vessels, Bottles, Flasks, Tankards, Plates	GMC Publications

Woodturning: A Foundation Course (New Edition)	Keith Rowley
Woodturning: A Source Book of Shapes	John Hunnex
Woodturning Jewellery	Hilary Bowen
Woodturning Masterclass	Tony Boase
Woodturning Techniques	GMC Publications
Woodturning Tools & Equipment Test Reports	GMC Publications
Woodturning Wizardry	David Springett

WOODWORKING

40 More Woodworking Plans & Projects	GMC Publications
Bird Boxes and Feeders for the Garden	Dave Mackenzie
Complete Woodfinishing	Ian Hosker
David Charlesworth's Furniture-Making Techniques	David Charlesworth
Electric Woodwork	Jeremy Broun
Furniture & Cabinetmaking Projects	GMC Publications
Furniture Projects	Rod Wales
Furniture Restoration (Practical Crafts)	Kevin Jan Bonner
Furniture Restoration and Repair for Beginners	Kevin Jan Bonner
Furniture Restoration Workshop	Kevin Jan Bonner
Green Woodwork	Mike Abbott
The Incredible Router	Jeremy Broun
Making & Modifying Woodworking Tools	Jim Kingshott
Making Chairs and Tables	GMC Publications
Making Fine Furniture	Tom Darby
Making Little Boxes from Wood	John Bennett
Making Shaker Furniture	Barry Jackson
Making Woodwork Aids and Devices	Robert Wearing
Pine Furniture Projects for the Home	Dave Mackenzie
Router Magic: Jigs, Fixtures and Tricks to Unleash your Router's Full Potential	Bill Hylton
Routing for Beginners	Anthony Bailey
The Scrollsaw: Twenty Projects	John Everett
Sharpening Pocket Reference Book	Jim Kingshott
Sharpening: The Complete Guide	Jim Kingshott
Space-Saving Furniture Projects	Dave Mackenzie
Stickmaking: A Complete Course	Andrew Jones & Clive George
Stickmaking Handbook	Andrew Jones & Clive George
Test Reports: The Router and Furniture & Cabinetmaking	GMC Publications
Veneering: A Complete Course	Ian Hosker
Woodfinishing Handbook (Practical Crafts)	Ian Hosker
Woodworking Plans and Projects	GMC Publications
Woodworking with the Router: Professional Router Techniques any Woodworker can Use	Bill Hylton & Fred Matlack
The Workshop	Jim Kingshott

UPHOLSTERY

Seat Weaving (Practical Crafts)	Ricky Holdstock
The Upholsterer's Pocket Reference Book	David James
Upholstery: A Complete Course (Revised Edition)	David James
Upholstery Restoration	David James
Upholstery Techniques & Projects	David James

TOYMAKING

Designing & Making Wooden Toys	*Terry Kelly*
Fun to Make Wooden Toys & Games	*Jeff & Jennie Loader*
Making Board, Peg & Dice Games	*Jeff & Jennie Loader*
Making Wooden Toys & Games	*Jeff & Jennie Loader*
Restoring Rocking Horses	*Clive Green & Anthony Dew*
Scrollsaw Toy Projects	*Ivor Carlyle*
Wooden Toy Projects	*GMC Publications*

DOLLS' HOUSES AND MINIATURES

Architecture for Dolls' Houses	*Joyce Percival*
Beginners' Guide to the Dolls' House Hobby	*Jean Nisbett*
The Complete Dolls' House Book	*Jean Nisbett*
The Dolls' House 1/24 Scale: A Complete Introduction	*Jean Nisbett*
Dolls' House Accessories, Fixtures and Fittings	*Andrea Barham*
Dolls' House Bathrooms: Lots of Little Loos	*Patricia King*
Dolls' House Fireplaces and Stoves	*Patricia King*
Easy to Make Dolls' House Accessories	*Andrea Barham*
Heraldic Miniature Knights	*Peter Greenhill*
Make Your Own Dolls' House Furniture	*Maurice Harper*
Making Dolls' House Furniture	*Patricia King*
Making Georgian Dolls' Houses	*Derek Rowbottom*
Making Miniature Gardens	*Freida Gray*
Making Miniature Oriental Rugs & Carpets	*Meik & Ian McNaughton*
Making Period Dolls' House Accessories	*Andrea Barham*
Making Period Dolls' House Furniture	*Derek & Sheila Rowbottom*
Making Tudor Dolls' Houses	*Derek Rowbottom*
Making Unusual Miniatures	*Graham Spalding*
Making Victorian Dolls' House Furniture	*Patricia King*
Miniature Bobbin Lace	*Roz Snowden*
Miniature Embroidery for the Victorian Dolls' House	*Pamela Warner*
Miniature Needlepoint Carpets	*Janet Granger*
The Secrets of the Dolls' House Makers	*Jean Nisbett*

CRAFTS

American Patchwork Designs in Needlepoint	*Melanie Tacon*
A Beginners' Guide to Rubber Stamping	*Brenda Hunt*
Celtic Knotwork Designs	*Sheila Sturrock*
Celtic Knotwork Handbook	*Sheila Sturrock*
Collage from Seeds, Leaves and Flowers	*Joan Carver*
Complete Pyrography	*Stephen Poole*
Creating Knitwear Designs	*Pat Ashforth & Steve Plummer*
Creative Doughcraft	*Patrica Hughes*
Creative Embroidery Techniques	
Using Colour Through Gold	*Daphne J. Ashby & Jackie Woolsey*
Cross Stitch Kitchen Projects	*Janet Granger*
Cross Stitch on Colour	*Sheena Rogers*
Designing and Making Cards	*Glennis Gilruth*
Embroidery Tips & Hints	*Harold Hayes*
An Introduction to Crewel Embroidery	*Mave Glenny*
Making Character Bears	*Valerie Tyler*
Making Greetings Cards for Beginners	*Pat Sutherland*
Making Hand-Sewn Boxes: Techniques and Projects	*Jackie Woolsey*
Making Knitwear Fit	*Pat Ashforth & Steve Plummer*
Needlepoint: A Foundation Course	*Sandra Hardy*
Pyrography Designs	*Norma Gregory*
Pyrography Handbook (Practical Crafts)	*Stephen Pool*

Ribbons and Roses	*Lee Lockhead*
Tassel Making for Beginners	*Enid Taylor*
Tatting Collage	*Lindsay Rogers*
Temari: A Traditional Japanese Embroidery Technique	*Margaret Ludlow*
Theatre Models in Paper and Card	*Robert Burgess*
Wool Embroidery and Design	*Lee Lockhead*

HOME & GARDEN

Home Ownership: Buying and Maintaining	*Nicholas Snelling*
The Living Tropical Greenhouse	*John and Maureen Tampion*
Security for the Householder: Fitting Locks and Other Devices	*E. Phillips*

VIDEOS

Drop-in and Pinstuffed Seats	*David James*
Stuffover Upholstery	*David James*
Elliptical Turning	*David Springett*
Woodturning Wizardry	*David Springett*
Turning Between Centres: The Basics	*Dennis White*
Turning Bowls	*Dennis White*
Boxes, Goblets and Screw Threads	*Dennis White*
Novelties and Projects	*Dennis White*
Classic Profiles	*Dennis White*
Twists and Advanced Turning	*Dennis White*
Sharpening the Professional Way	*Jim Kingshott*
Sharpening Turning & Carving Tools	*Jim Kingshott*
Bowl Turning	*John Jordan*
Hollow Turning	*John Jordan*
Woodturning: A Foundation Course	*Keith Rowley*
Carving a Figure: The Female Form	*Ray Gonzalez*
The Router: A Beginner's Guide	*Alan Goodsell*
The Scroll Saw: A Beginner's Guide	*John Burke*

MAGAZINES

WOODTURNING · WOODCARVING · FURNITURE & CABINETMAKING THE DOLLS' HOUSE MAGAZINE CREATIVE CRAFTS FOR THE HOME THE ROUTER · THE SCROLLSAW BUSINESSMATTERS

The above represents a full list of all titles currently published or scheduled to be published.
All are available direct from the Publishers or through bookshops, newsagents and specialist retailers.
To place an order, or to obtain a complete catalogue, contact:

**GMC Publications,
Castle Place, 166 High Street, Lewes, East Sussex
BN7 1XU, United Kingdom
Tel: 01273 488005 Fax: 01273 478606**

Orders by credit card are accepted